Fight for Grace

Fight for Grace

It's Time to Roll Up Your Sleeves

ANDREW NELSON

WESTBOW
PRESS
A DIVISION OF THOMAS NELSON

Unless otherwise stated all Scripture references are taken from the N.A.S.B version of the Bible.

WestBow Press books may be ordered through booksellers or by contacting:

WestBow Press
A Division of Thomas Nelson
1663 Liberty Drive
Bloomington, IN 47403
www.westbowpress.com
1-(866) 928-1240

ISBN: 978-1-4497-7340-3 (sc)
ISBN: 978-1-4497-7341-0 (hc)
ISBN: 978-1-4497-7342-7 (e)

Library of Congress Control Number: 2012920883

Printed in the United States of America

WestBow Press rev. date: 11/8/2012

For
Kristi

Deus maxima instrumentum gratia in vita.
Gratias mea!

"Andrew Nelson is a passionate defender of the gospel of grace. He is intimately acquainted with the love of Christ and longs for others to take hold of the same message that has transformed his Christian experience forever. This book is insightful, challenging, and most importantly, honoring to our Lord Jesus Christ. Read this book to abandon guilt and embrace God's grace. Read it to enjoy the rich, authentic relationship with Jesus that you never imagined possible."

ANDREW FARLEY
bestselling author of "The Naked Gospel" and "Operation Screwtape"
host, "Andrew Farley LIVE" on Sirius XM 131

"Andrew Nelson amazes me. He is a young man to whom God has given a nearly ridiculous understanding of the gospel, and he writes in a manner that expertly communicates the heart of God for people. His book, "Fight for Grace," is a thoroughly invigorating walk through the majestic beauty of God's love and ability for us. The reader cannot help but come away with a passion and yearning to fight for the gospel of God's grace as the highest treasure it is."

RALPH HARRIS, author of "God's Astounding Opinion of You," and President of LifeCourse Ministries.

"Is Jesus enough? If you are a Christian, the correct answer is "Yes!" But is that the real answer? Do you really believe that Jesus is enough for you? If you are asking these questions, welcome to the fight for grace. Andrew Nelson asked these questions. Life circumstances, disappointments and struggles pressed him for answers. In this wonderful book, he shares his journey to the answer "Yes!" – his fight for grace. Journey with him. You will be encouraged and find hope and strength for the battle."

BOB CHRISTOPHER
President
People to People Ministries

"It is always refreshing to find a book that is clear on the gospel and emphasizes living under grace. Andrew Nelson shows how these two are essentially related. The reader will find many things to stretch his or her appreciation of God's grace."

CHARLIE C. BING
Founder and Director
GraceLife Ministries

"Andrew provides us with a refreshing exegesis of God's wonderful grace, illustrated with his own openness and vulnerability as well as humor. He gives us a scriptural understanding that helps us put daily grace into practice. This quintessential approach to God's purposes for us here and now and the link between understanding grace and living in His love, make this book compulsory for every Christian struggling with guilt or the need for approval. It is an enjoyable book, stuffed full of practical implications for living in freedom and joy. If you want to better understand grace and the Holy Spirit's roll in your life, this is a must-read book. "

CARL BAKER
Pastor, Mission Village Christian Fellowship
San Diego, CA

"The real value of this book is that it is written by one who has moved from reliance on his own performance for spiritual vitality to a reliance on his relationship with the living triune God for his spiritual vitality."

DR. STEPHEN P. SAMMONS, Pastor, Lake Murray Community Church

"A very clear and stunning reminder of our security in the finished work of Christ......Jesus + Nothing = Everything we need"

JASON WINTERS
Worship Pastor, Mountain View Community Church
Ramona, CA

Contents

Foreword
By Jeremy White

My friend Andy Nelson has given us a tremendous gift in *Fight for Grace.*

I say this not based on how personally proud I am of him as his former youth pastor (although the truth of that cannot be denied). Instead, I say this based on watching Andy grow into one of the finest young communicators of the gospel of Jesus Christ that I have read among his generation of emerging leaders. This book is proof positive.

A fresh voice of grace and truth that is desperately needed in American church culture today, Andy insightfully challenges and lovingly corrects much of the subtle and not-so-subtle manipulation, legalism, and high-pressure tactics employed by well-meaning messengers in their quest to raise up a more passionately engaged generation of Christ-followers.

The truth is, spiritual *maturity* is the outgrowth of spiritual *security*, not vice versa. Only when a person understands, embraces, and begins to live in the awareness of their absolute security in Christ – regardless of external performance – will they begin to bear real fruit in this life. This is essentially what Christ was introducing when He taught His disciples the importance of "abiding" in Him (John 15).

Rather than challenging the church to be more radical – to suck it up and sacrifice until it hurts – Andy helps us learn to rest in the all-consuming, all-encompassing reality that Jesus is truly enough. We no longer have to live our lives on a desperate, existential quest to somehow "please God." Because of Christ, God is pleased – and that is the essence of the finished work of Jesus on our behalf. In *Fight for Grace*, Andy unpacks the "why" and clarifies the "how" so that we can begin to more fully take Jesus up on His offer: "Come to me, all who are weary and heavy-burdened...and you will find rest for your souls."

With theological integrity and pastoral care, this book puts the gospel of grace back in its proper place as not only the crux by which every believer is *saved*, but also by which every believer is called to *live!* Many Christians understand their salvation as the moment in time when they received their ticket to go to heaven someday. Until then, Christianity is little more than a white-knuckled ride of trying not to screw up too badly in the process of living life this side of eternity.

Jesus wants so much more for you! *Fight for Grace* will help illuminate these things to your heart and mind so that you can begin to embrace a Jesus more amazing than you ever thought possible – the Jesus of the Bible. Organizing the entire book around our relationship to the Triune God (Father, Son, and Holy Spirit), Andy offers us a journey well worth taking. You owe it to yourself to read this book, where you will discover the freedom you've always dreamed of but feared was too good to be true.

And one more thing: as someone who knows Andy well, I can assure you that as you read this book you will be journeying along with a person who understands the grace of God from a much deeper well than mere intellectualism. Andy's views are not only scriptural, but battle-tested in the field of life. He knows God's grace experientially. Having witnessed him survive and thrive through some heartbreaking challenges, failures, and trials, I want every reader to know that in Andy, they've got a friend familiar with suffering, loss, and pain. He's not some young, up-and-coming ivory tower type who writes because he loves to hear the sound of his own voice rattle in his head. Rest assured, this book is a labor of love for his fellow travelers.

Blessings upon your journey!

JEREMY WHITE
Lead Pastor
Author of "The Gospel Uncut"
Valley Church, Vacaville, CA

Preface

Fight for Grace has been a ten-year labor of love. Two of those years were spent writing the book, and the other eight were spent on an often-hellacious spiritual journey out of legalism and into grace. I have by no means "arrived," but I'm thrilled at who God has revealed Himself to be since my journey began.

This book contains what God put on my heart regarding the Christian faith and is designed to not only teach important truths, but to also make a dire plea for all Christians to "fight" or stand up for these truths.

I have divided the book into three parts, one for each member of the Trinity. Each part covers how a "fight for grace" has negatively impacted the image and work of each member of the Godhead, and will identify truths that will combat the lies we face daily. At the end of each chapter there are "Battle Strategies" to help you practically apply the truths covered in each chapter, so that gospel truth does not simply remain head knowledge, but is applied to everyday life.

There is a battle out there, and while Jesus is already the victor, it is crucial that the Church take its identity in Christ seriously and move to stand up for the amazing work of the Savior.

If we don't, then who will?

ANDREW NELSON
July, 2012

"Amazing grace, how sweet the sound,
That saved a wretch like me.
I once was lost but now am found,
Was blind, but now I see."

John Newton

Jesus Is Enough?

Two thousand years ago something extraordinary happened: God reached down into sin-ridden humanity to pave a path back to relationship with Him. Love was His fuel, and Jesus His instrument.

This Nazarene carpenter suffered unspeakable pain and anguish as He was ruthlessly flogged and crucified. As if the physical pain wasn't bad enough, the Father made Jesus, His perfect Son, to be sin. Exactly what this entailed will most likely forever remain a mystery, but we know that whatever it was, something brutal beyond words happened to the one Person who didn't have it coming to Him. Jesus absorbed the wrath of God for sins that He never committed and faced a death that He never deserved so that we could once again know the God who created us.

For centuries a war has existed over one simple word, a word that is at once subtle and powerful, life changing and challenging, liberating and joyous. This word is *grace*. Maybe you have heard of it. The Greek word for grace is *charis* and it means "unmerited favor." It is this word that the apostle Paul used when he stated, *"For by **grace** you have been saved through faith..."* (Ephesians 2:8). It is by God's completely free, undeserved, and unmerited favor that we are saved. This grace of God was poured from heaven onto earth when Jesus came and suffered for our sins. It is this grace that holds Christianity together like fine glue separating it from all man-made religions. Without grace, there is no Christianity.

This war over grace is the same war that Paul and the rest of the apostles spent so much time fighting during their ministries. The early churches often struggled with applying the practices of Old Covenant law to the New Covenant. While some practices of the law, like, circumcision, are not seen as issues for modern believers, we still struggle with whether Jesus is enough for us. This is why war still exists in the trenches of our pews and from the heights of our pulpits. This war has its origin not in some outside force, but in the deepest and most tender recesses of the human heart, where a simple question asks: *Is Jesus enough?*

The reality is that God did something amazing for us. He took it upon Himself to do the work that we ourselves could not do. He carried our sin, did away with it entirely, and gave us a chance to be freely in relationship with Him through simple faith in His Son. God's only expectation now for humanity is that His Son be received, that Jesus be *enough* for us.

But inside many church buildings today, we see a Jesus who isn't enough and a salvation that requires more than *His* work. Instead of faith in Jesus alone, we see a salvation that needs confession, communion, water baptism, good works, and other religious trappings. While we may not willingly admit it, too many of us have traded Jesus for religious duties. We have forgotten grace and are failing to fight for it like the apostles did.

We humans have a hard time accepting that which we feel is undeserved. We feel that we must earn grace or make ourselves worthy of it. We minimize Jesus' work because of this mentality, and the consequences are staggering. Religious bondage is in good supply in the modern Church.

Because Jesus is not seen as enough, our entire view of God has become radically skewed. If God is not *the* God of grace, then Jesus is not the awesome Savior that Scripture shows Him to be; the Holy Spirit is not the wonderful Helper who lovingly guides us daily; nor is the Father our Daddy to whom we can freely run any time of the day, and who completely accepts us because of the all-sufficient work of Jesus. Christians are left with a faith that produces not a living freedom in our relationships with God, but a pseudo-divine grace that binds us with rules and regulations that no honest person will ever be able to meet.

The world has enough religions where grace is absent, replaced by a tireless chasing after God. Jesus knew this and came to create something different and new. But does His vision continue? Are we living in grace? What is needed is not more man-made gods that require the impossible from us, but the God of Scripture. The God that Jesus came to reveal. *This* is the God that the world needs.

But how will the world hear about the grace of God if His children do not speak it? And how will His children speak it if they themselves do not *know* it?

I ask you, dear reader, is Jesus *enough* for you? How you answer this will show what side of the battle you are on, and whether you are helping or hindering the Gospel of God. The time of mixing the gospel with bondage must come to an end. Jesus is worth too much for it to continue.

It is time to fight for grace.

PART I

Fight for the Son

The burden of life is from ourselves,
its lightness from the grace of Christ and the love of God.

William Bernard Ullanthorne

One

Gone Baby Gone

gone
[gawn, gon]
adjective

1. Departed
2. Ruined
3. Deceased

Imagine this: you're a very poor and VERY indebted college graduate, and you desperately need a car to make the long commute to and from your new job. To make matters worse, your parents did not offer any help and you have absolutely no money of your own. Or you don't, that is, until one day when you are at home making your daily dose of rice and water and the doorbell rings. When you open the door, there is no one there. But there is an envelope at your feet. As you pick it up, you can tell that it is not a mere letter, but that it contains *something*.

Overflowing with enthusiasm at the notion that someone thought of you (you're a very lonely, indebted college student), you close the door and open the envelope. Inside is a letter and a key. Confused, you read:

> *Dear Sir,*
>
> *It has come to our attention that you owe a loan to our institution amounting to $75,000. For a graduation present, we have decided to pay your expenses for you. Your balance is now $0.00.*
>
> *In addition, it has come to our attention that you need a car. So it has been our great pleasure to give you this cobalt blue BMW 6 Series. We trust that you will find it sufficient for your needs. Also included is a gas card for your personal and convenient use. This you will find in the glove compartment beneath the free wax.*
>
> *Sincerely,*
> *Financial Aid*

Wow! Can you imagine? No debt, free car (super cool car at that), and a free gas card? *Beneath the free wax?*

But there's a second part to the story. After you receive the car and have had the pleasure of enjoying it for a while, you wake up one morning to a knock on the door. This time you find a policeman, who has come to tell you that your car, free wax and all, was stolen in the night.

Ouch. It was fun while it lasted. Now you have to work to afford a car again, and you have no way of commuting to your job. Feeling defeated, you forget about having your loans paid off and return to your breakfasts of rice and water.

So many Christians receive the good news of salvation with joy, seeing it as more than they could ever imagine – more than they ever thought they would need. But as time goes on, the grace of God slowly turns into religious bondage, as if it was stolen right from under their feet.

HEY YOU! WHERE DID YOU PUT MY GRACE?

It's sad to say, but a look into the lives and beliefs of many Jesus followers would reveal a faith that is full of everything but grace. The pews are full of Sunday morning churchgoers in desperate need of some good news, but more often than not church is where they go to get whipped back into shape instead of a place where they can celebrate Jesus. Instead of joy, they find sadness and depression; instead of freedom, bondage. Where peace is absent there is burden, and where love is not found there is bitterness and disunity. Instead of grace, there are rules and regulations.

So what exactly is happening to the people who profess the gospel, the good news of Jesus?

There are two possibilities about the source of the Church's discontent. The first is simple: Christians have a hard time understanding exactly what Jesus did for them. This is not hard to imagine. People love to complicate things, but the message of the cross is anything but complex. It reveals the heart of a God who truly and deeply cares for His creation and who would rather die than live without it forever. It reveals a salvation that is absolutely free and available to all through simple trust in the finished work of Christ for the forgiveness of sin and eternal life. Simplicity and accessibility are among the gospel's strong suits.

The second possibility is that Christians do understand the gospel, but they simply ignore it. This concept is more bothersome, but it's just as possible as the first. Truths such as grace are easy to accept but hard to live by. We may know intellectually about the grace of God, but living it out is a different beast.

The Apostle Paul affirmed that it's faith, or trust in Christ alone, that allows a person to enter into the blissful hereafter (Ephesians 2:8). Such a message can be a devastating blow to the ego of both the believer and unbeliever. It forces us all to admit the intolerable truth that it isn't our good works or religious duties that make us right with God or even *keep* us right with God. It is the blood of Jesus and nothing more.

Christians overshadow their knowledge that we truly didn't save ourselves with a long list of daily "religious" tasks that appear to keep them right with God; the truth that we are never more right with God than at the moment when we believe in Jesus is too much of a stumbling block. Yet this is the good news. The New Testament is infinitely clear on this point.

*"For by **grace** you have been **saved through faith**..." Ephesians 2:8*

*"For God so loved the world that he gave his one and only Son, that whoever **believes in him** shall not perish but have eternal life." John 3:16 NIV*

*"These things I have written to you who **believe** in the name of the Son of God, so that you may **know** that you have eternal life." 1 John 5:13*

*"He made Him who knew no sin to be sin on our behalf, so that we might become the **righteousness of God in Him**." 2 Corinthians 5:21*

That last one is a doozy. The righteousness of God? Really? Us? Simply through faith in Christ? Yes! God never intended it to be difficult for us to be saved. He loves us too much for that. This is grace.

So why aren't Christians resting? Why aren't we joyful? Why isn't every day a party?

Grace is gone, my friends. Gone baby gone. Stolen right from under our noses.

If you remove the undeserved favor of God, the gospel changes entirely. Instead of a gospel that leads to freedom, truth is replaced with a lesser, more burdensome pseudo-truth that is not the true gospel. The Apostle Paul said as much to the Galatian Church (Galatians 1:7).

The good news of Christ's crucifixion, burial, and resurrection for sinners is more than the *foundation* for our faith. It *is* our faith! *He* is our faith. If Jesus is not central to our Christianity, then there is no Christianity and there is no grace. He is everything for us. When a life is not resting in His work and love, it will be void of hope regardless of how religious in appearance it is.

God knew that we as a human race would never meet His perfect expectations. This is the whole basis of the New Covenant. God experienced enough human unfaithfulness under the Old Covenant to recognize that a New Covenant, or agreement for fellowship, was needed, one that was not based on our faithfulness to God but on His faithfulness to us. This is where Jesus came in. Because of His work on the cross, His gift needs only simple belief in order to be received. We enter into fellowship with God through faith in His Son's work.

Who would have thought that such a beautiful message would divide so many people within the Church? The very fact that there is a war over grace is proof that Satan has been busy. Very busy.

THE WAR

The war over the gospel of grace revolves around a simple question: *Is Jesus enough?* Is He enough not just for our salvation, but also for our lives afterwards? Or do we need to add to His finished work to make it suitable for us?

By definition Christians believe that Jesus is enough for salvation. We all recite the understanding that we were saved by "receiving Christ," or "trusting in Christ," or whatever similar verbiage we use. But when it comes to our actual lifestyles, there is too much "extra stuff" that gets thrown into our gospel. We are saved when we believe, but some of us say that we need to confess our sins to be forgiven. We are saved by faith, but some of us say that we won't be forgiven unless we forgive others. Jesus paid the final price for our sins, but after we are saved it's up to us to roll up our sleeves and get to work on "this Christian thing."

Somewhere between the freeing truth of the gospel and our lives as Christians exists this battle for grace.

Christ went through too much for humanity to add to His precious gift. The blood that pulsed through His veins and spilled to the ground on Calvary was pure. He did not deserve to go through hell for us, but He did. The best tributes we can give Jesus are lives lived in true response to His work, lives of rest in Him. Satan wants the exact opposite, and will do anything he can as a defeated being to distract us from Jesus' finished work. This is why we need to be ready to fight at a moment's notice.

TIME TO FIGHT

Many of us choose to opt out of the fight for grace, submitting to laws and religions of our own making instead of to the God who made us. Others of us have fought long and hard in the war and have taken about as many punches as we can; bruised and battered, we are busy recuperating in the spiritual ER. Then there are those who actively oppose grace, and who not only reject the idea of the grace of God, but who are imposing mindless religious ooze on top of it.

Perhaps our images of God and His gospel have been corrupted. To understand that Christians are one hundred percent right with God, that not only are we forgiven and cleansed from all unrighteousness (1 John 1:9) but that we *are* the righteousness of God (2 Corinthians 5:21) through simple faith in Jesus, is to believe the unbelievable! It is this good news that Jesus came to shout from the mountaintops.

Maybe you're reading this but don't buy into the whole "Jesus thing." Maybe you experienced Christianity already (or at least thought you did) and have had enough. But the search for peace and fulfillment evades no one, and is quenched only by receiving the Son of God. And so you're here, reading this book.

Jesus' claims are plain and simple:

*"The thief comes only to steal and kill and destroy; I came that they may have life, and have it **abundantly**." John 10:10*

God's will for our lives, whatever our backgrounds, is that we live life to the fullest, and Jesus is the means to that life. If you are experiencing anything less, then you are falling short of the Divine will.

If we believe a gospel that is anything but exclusively good, then we do not believe the real gospel of God. If our experiences with God or His church have been anything but freeing and full of love, then we are not experiencing the gospel of grace.

Now is the time for those who know the grace of God to roll up their sleeves and stand up for the grace that has disappeared from so many hearts. It is time for those who impose mindless religion to repent and teach the true grace of God. It is time to take back the grace that was stolen. We are doomed without it.

Battle Strategies

- Do you truly believe that Jesus' work is enough for your salvation? If you are a Christian, then by definition you should. But often we adopt religious practices that we believe will help us "get right" with God. When we do this we forget about *grace*.
- As you go through your day, be mindful of what you believe about the gospel. Are you relying on Christ's finished work, or on something else? Is His work enough for your right standing with God, or do you feel a need to "doctor it up" a bit?
- If you find that you're not resting in His finished work, take a few minutes to simply sit and do *nothing*. That's right, nothing! As you sit, thank Jesus that His work has allowed you to cease trying to please God. *Rest,* knowing that even if you stayed in *this place* for the rest of your life, God would love and accept you as His righteous child because of the work of His Son. This is a mindset truly honoring to the Savior's work.

Two

Crucifying the Gift

cru·ci·fy
[kroo-suh-fahy]
verb

1. To kill by nailing or binding the hands and feet to a cross
2. To treat with injustice
3. To persecute

The battle for grace begins and ends with a correct understanding of the person and work of Jesus. No other message exists today that causes more discussion or division than that of Jesus Christ. His claims, while simple, exude a reality that not many people – believers and unbelievers alike – are willing to receive. His message of salvation by grace through faith in Him does not contain one ounce of a "beating around the bush" mentality.

As simple as the message of salvation seems, it was largely rejected by the religious leaders of Jesus' day. This was partly because the Jews – a people who lived in bondage and whose nation had been constantly under siege – thought they were waiting for a Messiah to come and deliver them from the grip of their enemies (during the time of Jesus this was Rome). But instead of promising immediate physical deliverance, Christ focused on deliverance from a much deeper and more crucial bondage: one dealing not with enslavement to human enemies, but to the greater and more universal enemy known as *sin*.

The main religious leaders of Jesus' day were the Pharisees. These "experts" thought they had it all figured out; they did not wish to think of themselves as sinful. They were God's shining stars and most prized possessions. So when Jesus came along and told them that salvation was a gift based on belief in Him, and not on their "goodie two shoes" attitudes, He caused quite an uproar.

Maybe you've had, or heard, similar reactions to the gospel. Humans are the same today as they were during Jesus' time. We don't like admitting certain qualities that might expose our weaknesses. But receiving Jesus requires us to admit these things that we would probably rather not admit: the pettiness of our endless searching for fulfillment, our stubborn and selfish efforts to somehow earn or achieve true meaning; our ever-present moral shortcomings; and the crucial need we have for forgiveness. It even requires that we admit our deep and uncontrollable need to be with God and to have Him be a part of our lives. Often people will not even consider God unless tragedy strikes.

Vulnerable Infants

After the September 11 attacks in 2001, church attendance skyrocketed.[1] Exactly why is open to debate, but I suspect it had to do with the overwhelming sense of helplessness that much of the nation felt. We were all hit with the offensive knowledge that America was not the invincible land that we thought it was, and that it had a soft spot, a vulnerability that permeated every citizen

---

1 Barna Group. "The Barna Group - Barna Study Explores Faith in New York Since 9-11." The Barna Group - Barna Update. http://www.barna.org/faith-spirituality/516-barna-study-explores-faith-in-new-york-since-9-11 (accessed June 30, 2012).

within its borders. I suspect this was what drove many people to cry out to God. They needed answers, and something told them that they would find what they were looking for in God. As September 11 became part of the past, people slowly began to feel safer and more confident. Church attendance declined, and things pretty much went back to how they were.

Times like September 11 serve as a reminder of our vulnerability. But to really understand grace, we must realize that this side of us has always been there; we have never been anything other than vulnerable.

When we were infants we depended on the care of our parents for everything. As we grew older we learned to do some things for ourselves. We graduated from breast milk or formula to frozen pizzas, still paid for by someone else's paycheck and stored in someone else's fridge. Eventually we found (or will find) careers of our own, and we forgot our desperate need for someone else to provide everything for us. We got lost in the lie that we are in total control of our lives and are our own security.

When vulnerability is hidden, it's no surprise that the claims of Christ are attacked. To admit that Jesus was right is to admit that we *need* Him to save us. To do this is to admit that we are flawed, helpless, uncontrollably vulnerable, and without ultimate control over our lives. It forces us to face the fact that, like it or not, there is no certainty that this life is all there is, and that one day we could have to answer to God for our lives here on earth. And let's face it: none of us are squeaky clean!

The grace of God is not an easy concept to wrap the human mind around. History shows that this is true even for Christians, God's earthly representatives for His good news.

CRAZED GALATIANS

The Apostle Paul spent a great deal of his time rebuking and correcting young churches that had strayed from the gospel.

One such occasion is described in great detail in the book of Galatians.

A group known as the Judaizers had infiltrated the church and were propagating the idea that for a person to be a true Christian, they needed not only to trust in Jesus for salvation, but also to take up practices from the ceremonial laws of the Jews – specifically, the act of circumcision. Jesus was not enough for these individuals. His sacrifice was incomplete. Their belief system did not hold to the *sola fide* (faith alone) thrust of the teachings of Jesus and His good news to mankind, and so Paul wrote to admonish the false teachers and remind the Galatian believers of the true gospel.

In his letter Paul points out that the Judaizers were trying to corrupt the gospel of Christ by promoting a gospel that "really was no gospel at all" (Galatians 1:7 NIV). In Paul's eyes, any philosophy that said that salvation came from anything other than faith in the sufficient work of Jesus was a perversion of the truth and utterly damnable. Yet this mentality still exists today.

As many authors before me have noticed, the church seems at times to be losing the battle. Too many Christians today do not understand what it means to be saved "by grace through faith" and adopt false and damaging doctrines that teach a gospel other than the free gift spoken of in Scripture. Their mentalities do not accept Christ's sacrifice as sufficient for a right standing with God, and they often feel the need to add to Christ's gift with some sort of work.

Paul was absolutely clear: people are saved by grace (God's undeserved favor) through faith (trust) in the all-sufficient work of Jesus. God made it simple for us: grace alone through faith alone. Salvation is not something to be earned, but a gift to be accepted.

*"For by grace you have been saved through faith; and that not of yourselves, it is the **gift** of God..." Ephesians 2:8*

*"For the wages of sin is death, but the free **gift** of God is eternal life in Christ Jesus our Lord." Romans 6:23*

The Greek words for "gift" in both verses (*dōron* and *charisma,* respectively) have virtually the same definition: a free gift or present. If we change this free gift to anything that's not free, we have changed the gospel entirely.

The Galatian church added circumcision to the free gift. What qualifications have we added on ourselves and on others for a right standing with God?

We must be careful here. Satan's paralyzing lies make their way into our walks in more subtle ways that we can really imagine. The Galatian tragedy is by no means new and by no means less toxic than it was when Paul wrote the letter, and believers' responses to false gospels should be no less enthusiastic and passionate than Paul's:

"You foolish Galatians! Who has bewitched you?" Galatians 3:1 (NIV)

Paul even goes on to ask them how they received the Holy Spirit, the very Helper who guarantees their eternal life.

"This is the only thing I want to find out from you: did you receive the Spirit by the works of the Law, or by hearing with faith? Are you so foolish? Having begun by the Spirit, are you now being perfected by the flesh?" 3:2-3

Paul asks, "Was the gift of the Spirit that sealed your salvation and began your intimacy with God truly a gift or did you do something to earn it?" Of course it was a gift.

Paul knew the awful consequences of getting the good news wrong. Not only would people within the church in Galatia not find the abundant life that God would have them find, but the work of Jesus could not be magnified to its highest and most deserved place. The lost would hear a false gospel. Imagine the horrific consequences of getting the gospel wrong, not only for us as individuals, but for all the people that we might mislead.

OWING GOD

To truly understand this free gift of eternal life, something crucial must be understood about our relationship with God.

We do not *owe* God a thing.

So many Christians do not understand this. They live their lives in constant bondage believing that God is floating around "up there," waiting for them to repay Him for the gift of Jesus. Wounded souls wake up every day believing that they are in debt to God and that they must work hard to do good deeds if they are ever to become deserving of their salvation.

The reality, however, is far less burdensome and far more full of grace. Jesus' work allowed us to be completely *out of debt* to God. This was the whole point of Calvary.

As sinners, we owe an infinite amount of perfection to God that we could never repay. But Christ can – and did – pay for it two thousand years ago. Once we receive His gift, we are totally and completely and bountifully in the black with God! We owe Him nothing. Zero. Zilch. Nada.

The problem is that too many believers don't understand this part of the gospel, and consequently don't teach it to unbelievers. They make becoming a Christian look like an act of unending, and ever-tiring, penance, about as thrilling as receiving a colonoscopy.

A far cry from what Jesus had in mind.

UNCHECKED BELIEFS

What we believe about the gospel shows how we understand God. If what Jesus did was not enough for us to receive as a gift, then

God really is a demanding task master who gives His rebellious creation exactly what we deserve: life lived in the endless pursuit of unattainable salvation.

But if Jesus was – and is – enough, then God is far from the most demanding, most furious person we know. He is infinitely full of a boundless grace and endless love towards humanity that makes all other loves look like hatred.

The church needs to step up and figure out what God they are serving and what gospel they believe in. Otherwise, it will never have peace, and the world will forever be without the hope that Jesus offers.

The Jews crucified the Gift of God two thousand years ago, and the same temptation exists for us today. We can either accept the Nazarene carpenter who is God, or we can nail Him to a cross again by rejecting His gift. We can live our lives in celebration of the finished work of Christ, or we can make Christianity all about owing God. The choice is ours, but remember: our choice determines which side of the fight we are on.

Battle Strategies

- Jesus went through hell for us. Why did He do this? Because He knew that if we were to have any hope of salvation it had to be a *gift* based on *His* work. But like the religious leaders of Jesus' day, people often don't like being vulnerable enough to receive this type of gift. We prefer to place faith in our own achievements and abilities, instead of the person and work of Christ.
- In our society being vulnerable is often seen as "wimpy" or "weak," especially for men. But coming to Jesus *requires* us to admit our vulnerability. It *requires* us to have a need for Him to meet.
- If you are not experiencing the grace of God in your life, take time to think about how vulnerable you are to God and how "needy" you are for Him. Do you *need* the work of Jesus, or are you placing faith in something else for your righteousness (rightness) before God?
- Remember back to the place in the last chapter where you sat to rest in God's grace? Return to it. Take time to allow yourself to be needy for Jesus' work. Then, thank Him for it.

Three

Position of the Cross

po·si·tion
[puh-zish-uhn]
noun

1. Condition with reference to location
2. A place occupied or to be occupied
3. The appropriate place

I became a Christian when I was thirteen or so. I say "or so" because I was one of those people who anxiously and frantically prayed multiple salvation prayers, waiting for *something* to happen. Nothing did, or at least nothing happened that I could see.

I was drawn to the Bible, and as I read I found comfort in its words about God's love and grace. John 3:16 brought me peace and excitement; knowing that I was part of the world that God cherished was amazing.

But for every "John 3:16" verse there seemed to be another, more ambiguous verse that contradicted Jesus' freeing claims. I would get excited about God's "love for the world" and the "eternal life" available to everyone who received Jesus. Then I would read 1 John 1:9 and get confused and burdened about the state of my forgiveness. Then Matthew 6:15 and surrounding passages knocked my confusion out of the park.

"For God so loved the world, that He gave His only begotten Son, that whoever believes in Him shall not perish, but have eternal life." John 3:16

"If we confess our sins, He is faithful and righteous to forgive us our sins and to cleanse us from all unrighteousness." 1 John 1:9

"But if you do not forgive others, then your Father will not forgive your transgressions." Matthew 6:15

Do you see a problem? These cannot all be true. People are either forgiven through belief in Jesus or not. If the verses all apply to unbelievers, then where is the dependence on Christ's finished work? If they all apply to Christians, then what really happened at salvation? Were we just partially saved? Isn't the whole point of the gospel total forgiveness from Christ? My guess is that most of us were not initially taught a gospel that said "believe in Jesus and forgive your brother, then you will be saved."

I read all of the verses as though they applied to me as a Christian and became very confused. I didn't understand how I could be given eternal life through faith and then have to confess my sins for "cleansing" and "forgiveness," or why I would have to forgive to be forgiven. It all seemed contradictory. Either I was saved by grace or I wasn't.

What I didn't know was that my confusion was because of the grace war.

JESUS IN FOCUS

As a young Christian I was taught that I was completely and permanently saved when I came to belief in Christ. But I came up empty when I searched for meaning in those other, seemingly contradictory verses. Because of this, I lacked real joy in my faith.

God created our brains to analyze, and when puzzle pieces don't fit nicely together it causes problems for people who pay close attention. On one hand, I believed that God loved me and that I was saved because of what Jesus did; but on the other, I experienced anxiety surrounding the "unexplainable verses." I know I was not alone here.

Deep down, every Christian knows that they are saved by grace and totally forgiven at the moment of salvation. This is why coming to Christ is like opening up the best Christmas present ever. But then we read verses like those listed above, and we hear doctrine that is contradictory to the grace of Jesus, and the flame of excitement seems to diminish.

Without understanding the correct contexts of the Scriptures, we can fall into the trap of believing that we are saved by faith, but that we lose our salvation every time we sin, so we need to constantly confess our sins to be re-forgiven and re-cleansed while simultaneously forgiving others so that we can somehow make our way to heaven. (Whew.)

Hopefully you see the problem. When the sufficiency of Christ's sacrifice on behalf of sinners is not the focus of our faith, we believe a false gospel and *wrongly interpret Scripture*.

It takes bravery and honesty to admit that some of Jesus' earthly teachings contradict the gospel of grace as we know it today. How can this be the case? Was Jesus crazy? Did He really believe that we were not saved by simple faith in Him?

A LITTLE PERSPECTIVE, PLEASE!

I was leading a retreat for my church one weekend and asked the congregation where and when the New Covenant began in Scripture. Some said Christ's resurrection. Others said the first chapter of Matthew. Others were deep in thought. I explained to them that we often see Matthew 1 as the beginning of the New Covenant. Logically, then, we see all of Jesus' teaching as taking place under the New Covenant and thus applicable to us Christians today. But this is not the reality. Scripture makes it very clear that it is not His birth that began the new covenant. It was His *death*.

> *"For a covenant is valid only when men are dead, for it is never in force while the one who made it lives." Hebrews 9:17*

> *"And in the same way He took the cup after they had eaten, saying, "This cup which is poured out for you is the new covenant in* **My blood**....*" Luke 22:20*

Understanding this is key to understanding Scripture. If we don't understand when the New Covenant began and exactly what it is, then we will continually be confused by teachings of Jesus that seem to contradict the gospel. If we don't understand the New Covenant, then we will never understand the concept of being saved by grace through faith.

Jesus' teaching on earth had two main purposes. One was to prepare people for the new way that was to come, bringing grace through faith (the New Covenant). The other was to make human sin known in a deeper way. In theory, if the Jews knew just how deep and serious their sin issues were, then they would be able to more clearly see their need for a Savior and get saved.

We can use the following statements to help us understand Christ's teachings:

1. It is Jesus' death, not His birth, that began the New Covenant.
2. Christ's ministry on earth was done under the Old Covenant (Galatians 4:4).
3. Most of Jesus' teachings were designed to show people their need for God's grace.

Before we dive into this deeper, we need a proper perspective on the accomplishment of Christ on the cross.

JESUS SAT DOWN

God is unchanging, but the ways He deals with mankind have changed considerably. In the Old Testament, God's relationship with His chosen people was conditional on their faithfulness to Him. If they rebelled against Him and forgot about His Law, He would punish them in order to bring them back to repentance.

*"**If** you follow my decrees and are careful to obey my commands, I will send you rain in its season, and the ground will yield its crops and the trees of the field their fruit. Your threshing will continue until grape harvest and the grape harvest will continue until planting, and you will eat all the food you want and live in safety in your land." Leviticus 26:3-4*

*""But **if** you will not listen to me and carry out all these commands, and if you reject my decrees and abhor my laws and fail to carry out all my commands and so violate my covenant, then I will do this to you: I will bring upon you sudden terror, wasting diseases and fever that will destroy your sight and drain away your life. You will plant seed in vain, because your enemies will eat it." Leviticus 26:14-16*

In order to help the Jews maintain fellowship with Him, God set up sacrificial laws for the people to make atonement for their sins. In the daunting book of Leviticus this sacrificial system is written out in grueling detail, but in each case it was blood that bought forgiveness. The author of Hebrews recounts this as he tries to show his fellow Jews the finality of Christ's sacrifice.

*"And according to the Law, one may almost say, **all
things** are cleansed with **blood**, and without shedding
of blood there is **no forgiveness**." Hebrews 9:22*

It was always blood that brought God's forgiveness. Sin was a serious matter, and no amount of begging or bargaining with God would change His mind. If the people were guilty, Bessie the Goat's number was up.

But the problem was that God's forgiveness under the Old Covenant was never permanent, because the sins of the people were never permanently taken away. The blood of bulls and goats was never meant to take away sin (Hebrews 10:4). It could only *cover* it until the final sacrifice, Jesus, came.

Because of this, the Old Covenant Jews were in a continuous state of need to atone for sin. This only changed when Jesus arrived and stepped into the role of High Priest in order to make one final sacrifice for sin: Himself.

*"Every priest stands daily ministering and offering time after
time the same sacrifices, which can never take away sins; but He,
having offered one sacrifice for sins for all time, SAT DOWN
AT THE RIGHT HAND OF GOD...." Hebrews 10:11*

After offering Himself, Jesus sat down. His work was done. Such an act would have been unheard of for a human high priest, whose work was never done. There were always more sins to atone for. But now those in the line of Aaron were no longer responsible for the sins of the people. Jesus had shown up, and He completed the Jewish faith.

*"Let us fix our eyes on Jesus, the author and **perfecter**
of our faith, who for the joy set before him endured
the cross, scorning its shame, and sat down at the right
hand of the throne of God." Hebrews 12:2 NIV*

Jesus brought to completion, or "perfection," the plan that God began in the Israelites. He took away sin once and for all.

With no more animal sacrifices needed, every person who comes to Jesus can be totally and permanently saved.

> *"For by **one offering** He has **perfected** for all time those who are sanctified." Hebrews 10:14*

Sin made people imperfect. Jesus removed that imperfection by becoming the final sacrifice. Through Him believers are perfect again, because their sin is totally gone. In its place are forgiveness and righteousness, totally free gifts.

God's people no longer needed to have animal sacrifices to atone for their sins because their Messiah had come, a truth that many original recipients of the letter of Hebrews did not understand. When Jesus physically walked the earth, the Jews rejected Him. They wanted a military Messiah who would save them from Roman rule, but Jesus had other plans. He wanted to make them perfect in the eyes of God, without sin or blemish.

This is the heart of the New Covenant.

> *16 "THIS IS THE COVENANT THAT I WILL MAKE WITH THEM AFTER THOSE DAYS, SAYS THE LORD: I WILL PUT MY LAWS UPON THEIR HEART, AND ON THEIR MIND I WILL WRITE THEM,"*

He then says,

> *17 "AND THEIR SINS AND THEIR LAWLESS DEEDS I WILL REMEMBER NO MORE." Hebrews 10:16-17*

So why is this relevant? Because understanding forgiveness can help put confusing verses, such as 1 John 1:9 and Matthew 6:14-15, into perspective. If we understand New Covenant forgiveness, then we can read the Bible with the correct perspective, bringing every obscure verse under the captivity of God's amazing grace.

Battle Strategies

- Sometimes reading the Bible can be confusing. This is especially true when it comes to applying what we read to our lives today. But what is great about our God is that He is not out to confuse us. He simply wants us to know about His new way of doing things on this side of the cross. This *New Covenant* that began at Jesus' death is God's *final* means of relating to mankind. It is based solely on Christ's *finished* work and not on man's faithfulness to God, like the Old Covenant.

- A crucial aspect of this New Covenant is that God has forgotten the sins of His children. This is a hard concept to take in because we humans still remember our mistakes. But God does not work that way. He looks at the blood of Christ and is content to forget all of our sins at salvation. As you go about your life keep this in mind, especially if you sin. Instead of begging Him for forgiveness, simply thank Him for the work of His Son. Remember, it is blood that brings forgiveness, not your pleading. Keep His grace in focus.

Four

New Perspectives

new
[noo, nyoo]
adjective

1. Of recent origin
2. Odd and unfamiliar

I wasn't sure where I was exactly on a map, but I knew that, like Dorothy, I wasn't in Kansas anymore.

It was called the Atitaki Wilderness, and it was somewhere in central Canada. My dad had volunteered to lead my Boy Scout troop on a thirteen-day canoe trek into the deep Canadian wilderness. Then he volunteered me, too. We were dropped off twenty-five miles from civilization by a floatplane, and we had to make a rendezvous point in time for pick up.

The mosquitoes were intense, the beavers were abundant, and I was far away from my comfort zone. There were no movies, no video games, nothing but my dad, some Boy Scouts, and a few canoes. Because of the rugged landscape, we couldn't simply float down the rivers toward our destination. We had to portage (carry the canoe) around shallow riverbeds, wade through swamps, and even when we did get to use the canoes, we were forced off of the water constantly during thunderstorms (aluminum and electricity don't mix well).

That trip may not have seemed enjoyable to my twelve-year-old self, but in hindsight it gave me a view of life that I would never have seen from the comfort of my living room. My perspectives changed as I lived outside my comfort zone, battling the elements with my dad. Suddenly, life was not about being comfortable. It was about being uncomfortable and still making my home there.

I survived the trip (more like my dad kept me alive), and returned home a changed boy.

As we journey toward grace, there are many comfort zones to evade and numerous swamps to cross. We all have our ways of doing things, or beliefs that make us feel comfortable. But there are times when we must abandon the comfort of our traditions and step onto the bold path of following the real Jesus. He is not here to make us comfortable. He is here to take us on an epic adventure toward understanding that He is enough.

The problem is the more we allow Jesus to be enough for us, the more man-made religion we have to chuck away on the journey. And let's face it: this can be more terrifying than a lightning storm in an aluminum canoe.

SEE YOUR SIN!

Early in Jesus' ministry He ran into resistance from the Jewish officials, who obstinately expected the Messiah to bring a physical kingdom. But Jesus' kingdom did not begin in the physical; His was a spiritual journey. This is why Christ said that His kingdom was not of this world (John 18:36). The kingdom of God *begins* spiritually. Sure, there will be a time when Jesus comes back to bring a physical kingdom on earth, but He did not begin that way.

So when things got tense, what did Jesus do to get His followers to focus on a spiritual kingdom instead of a physical one taken by force? He taught them *perfection*.

Matthew 5, 6, and 7 consist largely of Jesus expressing the standard of perfection. The forgiveness passage of Matthew 6:14-15 is part of this.

*"For **if** you forgive others for their transgressions, your heavenly Father will also forgive you. But **if** you do not forgive others, then your Father will not forgive your transgressions." Matthew 6:14-15*

Notice the "if." Does that sound like the good news of grace through faith? No. And it shouldn't. That was not Christ's intention here. Remember, Jesus ministered under the Law, so He was teaching what perfection looked like under the Old Covenant.

The Old Covenant included the Ten Commandments, as well as the entire sacrificial system (think back to Bessie the Goat). The Law showed the people their sin, so that they would continually see their need for forgiveness and offer the blood of animal sacrifices to receive it. Paul, once a leading member of the Jewish community, describes his own personal response to the Law:

What shall we say then? Is the Law sin? May it never be! On the contrary, I would not have come to know sin except through the Law; for I would not have known about coveting if the Law had not said, "YOU SHALL NOT COVET." Romans 7:7

Paul is not saying that he didn't know what coveting was until he read the Law. What he is saying is that he didn't know the *depth* of sin until he read it in the Law.

"But sin, taking opportunity through the commandment, produced in me coveting of every kind…" Romans 7:8

Sin is by nature opposed to God's truth. Because the Ten Commandments represent the perfect standard of God's truth, sin takes a hold of an individual to produce "coveting of every kind." Where Paul might have struggled with one type of coveting before he knew the Law, after he saw the command, he struggled with all types of coveting.

The Law holds the whole world accountable to God's standards. It is His measuring stick for humanity. It is a legal "document" that shows two certain truths: first, that God's standard is perfect; and second, that humans fail miserably to meet this standard and need help. Jesus is this help, and ultimately, the Law acts as a helper to point the way to Christ.

> *"Why the Law then? It was added because of transgressions, having been ordained through angels by the agency of a mediator, **until the seed** would come to whom the promise had been made." Galatians 3:19*

> *"Therefore the Law has become **our tutor** to lead us to Christ, so that we may be justified **by faith**." Galatians 3:24*

The Law's final purpose was to point the way to salvation. Once the depth of sin is revealed, everyone can know his or her need to be justified by faith in Christ. By faith? Not by forgiving people or confessing our sins? Yes, by faith alone.

Over time, the Jewish people's belief in the Law had turned into serious legalism instead of acting as a reminder of sin. Jesus needed to get the people around Him to think about being perfect from the inside out, even beyond the standard shown by the Law.

The Law had become a way to gain a right standing with God, and the Jews needed to see that God's perfection was not just in the letter, but in the spirit. God's people couldn't keep the Ten Commandments and call themselves square with Him. They needed to be perfect from the inside out. This is why Christ takes the Divine perfection represented in the Ten Commandments to a deeper level in His teachings in Matthew 5, 6, and 7. Here are a few from chapter 5.

> *""You have heard that it was said, 'YOU SHALL NOT COMMIT ADULTERY'; but I say to you that everyone who looks at a woman with lust for her has already **committed adultery** with her in his heart." Matthew 5:27-28*

> *"But I say to you that everyone who is angry with his brother **shall be guilty** before the court; and whoever says to his brother, 'You good-for-nothing,' shall be guilty before the supreme court; and whoever says, 'You fool,' **shall be guilty enough to go into the fiery hell." Matthew 5:22**

To come to Christ, people need to realize that they cannot ever be perfect on their own. They need *grace* to be perfect (cleansed from sin). This is why Christ bled. As we read the New Testament it is extremely important to know that Jesus was born under the law and that the New Covenant did not begin until His death. The majority of the gospel stories describe Christ teaching *under the law*. Galatians 4:4 summarizes:

> *"But when the fullness of the time came, God sent forth His Son, born of a woman, born under the Law..." Galatians 4:4*

Grace through faith was the plan, but Jesus did not only teach grace through faith. He taught what *needed* to be taught so that people would eventually receive His grace.

SIN FREEING SOAP

So if believers are perfectly forgiven, then why do we need to "confess our sins?" John is very clear about believers confessing their sins to God in order to be forgiven, isn't he? And we can't take 1 John 1:9 and say that it's an Old Covenant teaching, because John wrote the letter *after* Christ's death.

Christians have used this passage for centuries as the proverbial "bar of soap" for when we mess up. But that was not John's intention. So what exactly is the occasion of this mysterious verse?

If we read all of 1 John with the understanding that we are saved by grace through faith, then understanding 1 John 1:9 becomes fairly simple. But before we get into this, I want to highlight something else. If 1 John 1:9 applies to believers, and Christians must confess their sins to be forgiven, then every time we commit a sin, *we lose our salvation*. Take a look:

> *"If we confess our sins, He is faithful and righteous **to forgive us our sins** and to cleanse us from **all unrighteousness**."*

Now hold on. Christians by definition are a forgiven and righteous people. We are as righteous, or "right" with God, as Jesus (2 Corinthians 5:21). So if we need forgiving and cleansing from *all* unrighteousness every time we sin, then we have the power to move back and forth from hell-bound to heaven-bound perhaps hundreds of times a day. Is this what God had in mind for us? Would the God who claims that His "yoke is easy" and "His burden light" (Matthew 11:30) create a system that is anything but easy and light? He would not.

God already battled with human unfaithfulness under the Old Covenant, and He does not intend to repeat this battle. This is why the New Covenant is structured around *His* faithfulness towards us, not the other way around. Remember, *His* work is enough to perfect all believers in Christ. This is not behavioral perfection. It is spiritual identity.

So what was John talking about with this letter? He was addressing a church under attack by a group of Gnostics who promoted a false gospel. Gnostics believed, among other things, that the flesh was evil. Because of this, they believed that Jesus did not literally come in the flesh as a man, but was a spirit. Further, they stated that a person could sin as much as he or she wanted and have no consequence, because the evil flesh was left to decay after death.

These false teachings are precisely what John was combating in his letter. He writes to two audiences: true believers (those in the light) and false teachers (those in the darkness). He continues this contrast of dark and light by pointing out several defining characteristics of people in the light and people in the dark.

*"If **we** say that we have fellowship with Him and yet **walk** in the darkness, **we lie** and do not practice the **truth**; but if **we** walk in the **Light** as He Himself is in the Light, **we** have **fellowship** with one another, and the blood of Jesus His Son **cleanses us from all sin**. If **we** say that we have **no sin**, we are deceiving ourselves and **the truth is not in us**. If **we confess** our sins, He is faithful and righteous to **forgive us** our sins and to cleanse us from **all unrighteousness**. If **we** say that we have not sinned, **we** make Him a liar and His word is not in **us**."* 1 John 1:6-10

It is easy for modern believers to read the "we" in this passage and apply it to the "we" that we know best: ourselves. But John was writing to a very specific group of people who needed to be identified as of God, or not of God. For the early church battling false teachers, this letter would help in their battle to distinguish who was of God and who was not, and it would also serve as an invitation for those who "claimed to be without sin" to "confess their sins" and be "forgiven and cleansed from all unrighteousness." There is only one group that matches the latter purpose: the unsaved Gnostic teachers.

I don't believe that anyone is truly unaware of their own sins, but we can certainly be in denial of them, and without an initial acknowledgement of sinfulness, salvation is not possible. John wanted those misled folk to recognize their sins and get saved.

EVERYTHING IS CHANGED

The cross did not just change a few things. It changed *everything*! Understanding this is crucial to correctly understanding the New Covenant and Christ's teachings before its inception. Because it was Christ's blood that initiated the New Covenant (Hebrews 9:15-22), Christ lived and taught under the Law (Galatians 4:4). We must remember this as we strive to take our understanding of Scripture captive to Christ and His work on the cross.

As we read Scripture, context is always king, especially when it comes to recognizing the New Covenant. When we don't truly understand God's way of doing things, the gospel life we live will be hindered by misapplication of God's word.

Jesus' teachings before the cross prepared the people of the day for faith and trust in Him. Verses such as Matthew 6:14-15 prepared for the New Covenant. They show the depth of God's perfection and how it supersedes even what the written Law states, as well as how miserably short we fall of this standard.

1 John 1:9 is a unique verse. You won't find any other New Testament epistle verses that command people to confess their sins to God *for forgiveness*. The rest of the Bible is full of the total forgiveness that everyone can have because of Jesus' amazing work. John's purpose was simply to help us understand the need for the initial forgiveness from sin.

Does this sound too good to be true? Welcome to grace. It's not hard to see why it's attacked. The enemy wants God's children to live in bondage, so he does everything he can to keep us from living out our freedom in Christ. He even uses our own pastors and church leaders to do it at times.

We must know the truth and fight for it. We must, above all else, leave the comfort of our living rooms and brave some Canadian swamps.

Battle Strategies

- It is crucial for us to understand that Jesus' sacrifice was enough for total forgiveness for all sin. As Christians, we do not need to confess our sins, and we certainly do not need to forgive people so that we can be forgiven.
- Initially confessing (agreeing with God) about our sin is crucial for salvation. After all, how will we be saved unless we know what we need to be saved from? But after we are forgiven, we no longer need to confess our sins for forgiveness. Talking to God about our struggles is important, and we *can* tell God our sins. Just don't expect Him to know what specific sins you are talking about because to Him they are *forgotten.*
- Forgiving those who have hurt us is very important, but our own forgiveness before God does not depend on it. This side of the cross we forgive because *we have been forgiven* (Colossians 3:13, Ephesians 4:32). As you reflect on how God has forgiven you consider giving the same forgiveness towards others. You will be surprised just how freeing this can be.
- As you read the Bible, use discernment when applying verses to your spiritual walk. If you do not read scripture with a New Covenant perspective on forgiveness, then you will likely be confused.

Five

Defanged

de·fang
[dee-fang]
verb

1. To cause to become less threatening
2. To render harmless

My friend Carl was possessed by a demon when he was a child, and no one knew exactly how it had happened, not even Carl. The only eyewitnesses were two people in the church he was visiting and their son (we'll call him Steve). Apparently, sometime during the service Steve's father decided that Steve was demon possessed. So the father grabbed him and started shaking him, trying to chase the demon away.

While he was shaking, Steve's mom reported seeing the demon jump out of their son and head for Carl.

"The demon's got Carl!" she cried. So her husband released his kung-fu grasp on Steve and scrambled over to Carl. Grabbing my friend's forehead, he began shaking him in hopes of being rid of the demon. After a few shakes Steve's dad let go.

Carl, meanwhile, didn't feel any different than usual, apart from a little fear at possibly becoming the host of Dwayne Demon and a slight headache from all the shaking. But he left church that day scared and confused.

Looking back many years later, Carl laughs at the story. He knew that he wasn't possessed, but as a young believer this was a terrifying experience for him.

I wish I could say that Carl's story is unique, but it isn't. Churches around the world differ with where to put Satan in their spiritual understandings. Some are quick to call every pain in life Satanic and every bush to be concealing a demon. Others ignore Satan completely, choosing to live in ignorance about his existence and work in the world around us. In *The Screwtape Letters*, C.S. Lewis highlights the fine line that we must walk:

"There are two equal and opposite errors into which our race can fall about the devils. One is to disbelieve in their existence. The other is to believe, and to feel an excessive and unhealthy interest in them. They themselves are equally pleased by both errors and hail a materialist or a magician with the same delight." C.S. Lewis, *The Screwtape Letters*

The war over grace that we see on earth is only a partial expression of what is going on in the spiritual realm. God does have a chief adversary, a fallen angel named Lucifer or Satan. He is the one who deceived Adam and Eve (Genesis 3), afflicted Job (Job 1:8), sought to destroy the work of Jesus by betraying him through Judas Iscariot (John 13:27), and who seeks to diminish the work of Christ in the lives of all people.

Believe it or not, Satan is a vicious reality. But what place does he have in the life of a believer? An unbeliever? Exactly how is Satan operating today, this side of the cross?

CRIPPLED PRINCE

Select churches and groups within Christianity believe that Christians can be demon possessed, or at least strongly harassed by demons. These beliefs often lead to much fear and legalism, as church members study their lives to find out if Satan has his grasp on them in one area or another.

But such suggestions seem to imply a dramatic conclusion: *God's work in the lives of His children can somehow be overpowered by the prince of darkness himself.* Not only does this have serious implications about how a person views God and His saving work in their life, but it raises Satan to a place of supreme power, a place that a cursory look at the Bible would reveal has always been his goal.

> [12] *"How you have fallen from heaven,*
> *O star of the morning, son of the dawn!*
> *You have been cut down to the earth,*
> *You who have weakened the nations!*
> [13] *"But you said in your heart,*
> *'I will ascend to heaven;*
> ***I will raise my throne above the stars of God,***
> ***And I will sit on the mount of assembly***
> ***In the recesses of the north.***
> [14] *'I will ascend above the heights of the clouds;*
> ***I will make myself like the Most High."*** *Isaiah 14:12-14*

Satan sought more power than God had given him. He wanted to make himself *like God* by striving in his *own power*. He tempted Adam and Eve the very same way, telling them that they would be like God if they ate from the tree of knowledge (Genesis 3:5). It was, of course, unreasonable. But reason was never Satan's strong suit. Pride was, and continues to be, his fuel, and he used it effectively until Christ came. On this side of the cross he stands *completely defeated* by the blood of Christ.

That's right. Because of the work of Christ, Satan is one hundred percent defeated.

> *"Now judgment is upon this world; now the ruler of this world will be **cast out**." John 12:31*

> *"...and concerning judgment, because the ruler of this world has been **judged**." John 16:11*

> *"When He had **disarmed** the rulers and authorities, He made a public display of them, having **triumphed over them through Him**." Colossians 2:15*

So what is happening in the church today? We all read the same Bible, and yet we seem to end up in vastly different places with regards to spiritual warfare. For the most part we agree that Satan is at work in the world and that spiritual warfare is a very real beast that we all deal with in one way or another. But what does that look like?

I've heard foreign missionaries tell stories of people under the possession of demons who levitated and did all types of otherworldly things that humans shouldn't be able to do. If you too have heard stories like these, you may have thought, "Okay, if Jesus has defeated Satan, then why can he still make people levitate?" This is well worth looking into.

Satan does exist, and he is at work in the world today, but Scripture tells us he has been "driven out," "condemned," and "disarmed." Satan has been defanged.

It is so easy to picture Satan and his goons as these big, ferocious beasts with plates of steel armor and sharp, serrated teeth. But that picture does not fit a "disarmed" host of evil ones. To come close to what he looks like now, we need to picture Satan and his goons as we just did, except stripped completely naked, without armor, and defanged of those insidious choppers. Sure, he may still have a growl, but once we look at what is growling at us, the intimidation will be over.

Satan is like an ant standing in front of a big spotlight. He casts a mean shadow, but is only three millimeters tall.

So how does a totally defanged devil work in the world today? It has everything to do with ownership.

Who's Yo Daddy!

Before I was saved, I used to get into arguments with a close friend over the validity of Christianity. He would be adamant that Jesus was the only way to God, and that certain lifestyles were sinful. I didn't agree. I remember getting so frustrated with him that I dragged in other friends and ganged up on him in our religious disputes.

I mean really, how stupid could he be to believe in Jesus and the Bible? *What a dufus.* All religions ultimately led to the same place, and anyone who said otherwise was a religious zealot worthy of a major bashing.

I knew I was right, until my dad started reading me the Bible and praying with me. And until I began going to a church and hearing the pastor talk about Jesus. Little by little, my heart began to change, and suddenly my buddy's claims didn't seem so weird. In fact, they started making sense.

I didn't realize it until years later but during those arguments with my friend, I was blind and naïve to the truths of God. I had been duped by the Dark Prince himself. The Bible says that this is Satan's power over the unbelieving world.

*"The god of this age has **blinded** the minds of **unbelievers**, so that they cannot see the light of **the gospel** of the glory of Christ, who is the image of God." 2 Corinthians 4:4 NIV*

Since the beginning of time, Satan has been hard at work, taking every willing eye off of God and onto himself. He did it in heaven before he was cast down, and he does it now.

Those people who reject Christ do so because Satan blinds them and keeps them in spiritual captivity. This is his chief power over unbelievers.

*"Those who oppose him he must gently instruct, in the hope that God will grant them repentance leading them to a knowledge of the truth, and that they **will come to their senses and escape from the trap of the devil, who has taken them captive to do his will.**" 2 Timothy 2:26*

Shocking? Yes. I agree that this is a harsh reality, but it is what is all around us. We are all owned by someone, God or Satan, and Satan has the power to do what he will with those people whom he owns. Even levitation, as those foreign missionaries described.

This is one of the chief reasons that the world is such a terrible place today: wars, famines, murder, adultery, incest, rape...the list goes on and on. Such acts are from a world that is under the control of Satan.

*"We know that we are of God, and that the whole world lies in the **power of the evil one.**" 1 John 5:19*

So what is the answer? How does one overcome the power of the Evil One? Thankfully, grace has an answer for us: Jesus. As dark and dreary as the outlook on humanity might be, there is hope in the gospel. Through Jesus Christ, believers are rescued.

*"For He **rescued** us from the domain of darkness, and transferred us to the kingdom of His beloved Son..." Colossians 1:13*

When we receive Jesus, we are taken from the slavery of Satan in *his* kingdom and placed under the freedom of Jesus Christ in

His kingdom. When I eventually accepted Christ, Satan lost a battle that he had been fighting my whole life. Little Andrew Nelson, the boy whom God loved, was rescued from Satan's grasp and made a blood-bought Saint of God. My Abba chased me down.

Looking back, I can see several events in my life that Satan meant to be bad, to keep me in slavery. Grade school teasing, my parents' divorce, even my own divorce and subsequent involvement in an unhealthy relationship, were all meant to distract me from a life lived to the absolute fullest in Christ. But nothing kept me from my salvation, and nothing has defeated me since. Sure, I experience trials that could be from Satan, or that might be simply natural for this life. But as a believer I can face those trials from the standpoint of *total victory.*

The apostle John wrote this to encourage young men in the church who were undergoing tribulations because of the Gnostic teachers infiltrating their churches. Check out his loving and assuring words:

> *"I have written to you, fathers, because you know Him who has been from the beginning. I have written to you, young men, because you are strong, and the word of God abides in you, and you have **overcome** the evil one." 1 John 2:14*

John knew that the churches undergoing trials needed some huge encouragement, and specifically that the young men, many of whom he may have known, needed reassurance that they had already won the victory over Satan through the victorious work of Jesus Christ. They needed the reminder that their God had appeared in order to "destroy the devil's work" (1 John 3:8). Jesus (the Word) lived in them, and they were completely safe.

Believers have overcome the devil through faith in Jesus. Satan cannot harm believers. They are kept safe.

*"We know that anyone born of God does not continue to
sin; the one who was born of God keeps him **safe**, and
the evil one cannot **harm** him." 1 John 5:18 NIV*

Have you ever thought of yourself as safe from the Devil?
The Greek word for "safe" is *tēreō,* meaning to "protect from
injury" or to "watch out for," and the Greek word for "harm" is
haptō, meaning "to latch onto, to touch." The message that John
was conveying to these early churches is the same universal truth
available to us today. Because we have been set free from sin, we
are protected from Satan's direct harm. Jesus as the "one who was
born of God" continually protects us. Satan cannot steal us from
God's grasp.

Free From Sin

A life of habitual sin is strong proof of Satanic ownership. But
believers are no longer characterized by sin because "God's seed"
(nature) remains in them.

*"No one who is born of God practices sin, because His seed abides
in him; and he cannot sin, because he is born of God." 1 John 3:9*

This is true in the sense that believers are completely righteous
at our cores, as well as what our lives look like after our salvation.
Sure, we all struggle in many ways and we will not behave perfectly
until heaven. But believers' lives are not dominated by sin because
we are no longer compatible with it. We have been *set free from
sin*, and are set free from the ownership of the Devil. We are now
owned or adopted, by our God.

*"Or do you not know that your body is a temple of the Holy
Spirit who is in you, whom you have from God, and **that you
are not your own?** For you have been **bought with a price:**
therefore glorify God in your body."1 Corinthians 6:19-20*

Believers belong to God. We are His children and are precious to Him. Can you imagine a loving Father allowing Satan to bring direct harm to his children? Absolutely not! Our heavenly Father loves us more than we can imagine. We may not feel or experience this love all the time, but it is there in full force. We are redeemed children of Abba.

Psalm 23 describes what it must look like to have a loving Father keeping watch over us.

> *"Even though I walk through the valley of the shadow*
> *of death, I fear no evil, for You are with me; Your rod*
> *and Your staff, they comfort me." Psalm 23:4*

God has our backs, and He is carefully watching over us with a mighty rod to beat away any wolves. He is our protector, and we are secure in Him.

The deciding factor in all of this is simple: are you owned by God or by Satan? If you are an unbeliever, then Satan has a hold on your life. But if God owns you, then God has your protection and security covered, and Satan cannot bring any direct harm to you. Any other belief system adds unnecessary burden to the grace of God and overlooks the work of Christ, putting the spotlight right on Satan.

Some of you may be thinking, "Okay, Nelson, I get it, but what about the spiritual warfare in my own life? What about those times when I was flooded with impure thoughts or dreams?"

You are not alone. I am in the same battle.

Battle Strategies

- The existence of Satan is a dark reality for our world today. Some people choose to ignore or disbelieve his existence, while others seem to focus on him too much. Scripture is clear that Satan *does* exist. However, he exists as a *defeated* being.
- Jesus has victory over the enemy. Because of this, the Children of God share this same victory. Satan cannot touch or attach himself to us. God owns us, and He is not willing to share.
- Consider whether you are victorious over Satan. If you are in Christ, then your victory is total. Rest in this and try to not blame every hardship in life on Satan. That gives him too much credit. There are other forces at work in this fallen world and hardships often exist because of this. Also, double check what you believe about his capability to do evil to you. Do you believe that you can be possessed or strongly harassed even if Christ has *defeated* the Evil One?
- If you have not yet done so, take time to consider trusting in Christ for your forgiveness and right standing with God. This is a sure way to go from the darkness of Satan to the glorious kingdom of God.

Six

Inner Battles

in·ner
[in-er]
adjective

1. Situated within or farther within
2. More intimate or secret

There it was, right out in the wide open: a pile of cash. It was a day's worth of transactions, ready for deposit, at the store where I used to work. In an instant the thought was there: *steal the money*! No one was in the room except for me, and I could take a little extra home to my wife.

Of course I immediately resisted the thought; I walked right past the money and back into the main floor where there were people in abundance. But this is just one time when a sinful thought has entered my mind (and it's one of the tamest thoughts I have had). Still it makes me wonder: where did that thought come from?

Before we take a look at Satan's work in the lives of believers, we need to understand something: Christians are *not* free from sin or its effects. Yes, we are free from sin's *hold* on our lives, and we have become willing slaves to righteousness (Romans 6:18). But sin is still present in our bodies and minds, complete with its own motives and desires.

> *"Therefore do not let sin reign in your mortal body*
> *so that you obey its lusts..." Romans 6:12*

That's right. *Its* desires. Not yours and not mine. Have you ever had an evil thought that seemed to come out of nowhere? Maybe it was to commit adultery or even murder someone. Where did *that* come from? Welcome to sin.

The reality is that deep within us we still carry the rebellion that was born in Adam and Eve. We carry the beast that is rape, incest, lust, hatred, and all other evils. So we shouldn't be surprised when we have evil thoughts, no matter how vile they may be. They come from within us.

A large number of the struggles we experience with our thought lives stem from the sin living in us. We have sexual or even violent dreams that seem to come from nowhere, and we wake up in the middle of the night thinking, "Why did I dream that? What is wrong with me? Where did that thought come from?"

While these could be images from Satan, the more likely answer is that they are *proof of sin living in us*. We give Satan credit for something that ultimately is not directly from him, but from *within us*. When we do this, it is not hard to conclude that the Dark One has a hold on us, when nothing could be further from the truth.

Another issue that believers fight with is the flesh (Galatians 3:3, 5:19-20). As Andrew Farley points out in his book *God Without Religion*, flesh is "the policies of the previous administration"[2] That is, the leftover ways of thinking encouraged by our past bondage to sin.

---

2 Farley, Andrew. "17." In *God without religion: can it really be this simple?*, 143. Grand Rapids, MI: Baker Books, 201163.

Because we have not received our new bodies yet, our brains are still recovering from a life lived under the slavery of sin. We each spent a certain number of years as slaves to sin, and that trained our brains to react in sinful ways. This *attitude* of living independently from God is the flesh. We still have the flesh, but like sin, it is *not* us. As new creations we have the exciting road ahead of living out of our *new identity* and striving to renew (teach) our minds the Godly way of living.

> *"And do not be conformed to this world, but be transformed by the renewing of your **mind**..." Romans 12:2*

There is much unlearning and learning to be done as we seek to live out who we are as Christians, being transformed by the renewing of our *minds* (thoughts, emotions, will, behavior).

We have sin in us, but are no longer its slave. This does not keep it from acting out at times through the flesh, yet this acting out is not from Satan. It is from *within* us. Because Christ lives in us and God owns us, Satan has no way of creeping inside of our bodies to influence us.

Does this leave out the possibility of Christians being demon possessed? Let's see: we are redeemed Children of God with Jesus living in us, and God our Abba looking out for us. I would say this is fairly self-explanatory. Satan's attacks on the Christian are external in nature and cannot come from deep within.

THE LIAR

The Bible tells us that Satan is the king of lying. In fact, he does nothing *but* lie.

> *"You are of your father the devil, and you want to do the desires of your father. He was a murderer from the beginning, and does not stand in the truth because there is **no truth***

> ***in him.*** *Whenever he speaks a lie, he speaks from his own nature, for he is a liar and the father of lies." John 8:44*

Catch that? There is no truth in him, none whatsoever. So what does he speak? Lies. When he lies, he does what he does naturally.

Satan's lies are *the chief means of spiritual warfare at work on believers today.* His lies are everywhere. Remember, he owns the world, so it is no surprise that his words permeate our society: girls are not pretty unless they look a certain way, guys are not guys if they show tenderness and emotion, abortion is a woman's right and thus should be allowed and encouraged, marriage is not permanent, adultery is justifiable, sex before marriage is necessary to see if the relationship will work in the long term. The list goes on and on.

But the lies do not exist only in generalities. They can be specific and affect our lives in personal ways. For example, growing up I was teased relentlessly at school. "You're gay" or "queer" would be words thrown at me. Of course, these accusations did nothing to inspire confidence in my masculinity. They damaged me, and they caused me to question the very essence of who I was as a man, including my sexuality.

Satan began attacking my masculinity at a very young age, trying to convince me that I was something that I wasn't. This led me to anxious introspection, wondering if I really was gay, whatever that meant. Before I knew it, I was labeling things about *myself* as gay. Satan continued to use this weak spot to attack me throughout my teen years. But God has done a mighty work in His Son to show me who I truly am to Him, so today the power of the lie has been broken in my life. My testimony is an example of how a lie can penetrate and affect a life. Of course, that was not the only lie that Satan told me, but it proved to be one of the chief battles I fought over the years.

When lies come at us, regardless of their flavor, *they are from Satan.* Sometimes it may be a direct lie whispered to us from demons; other times it may be indirect lies that we hear from the world. Either way, if it violates God's truth found in His word, it is a lie and is ultimately from Satan.

The crucial truth to remember is that Satan is limited in what he can do to believers. He cannot attach himself to or touch a believer. Jesus forbids it! But Satan can lie.

I have gotten myself into trouble analyzing "spiritual attacks" to see whether they are from Satan or not. I've always been an anxious person, so if my brain senses that there is even a chance that a demon is hovering over my head poking at me, I will take the thought and run with it. But focusing on Satan is never encouraged in the Bible. Our eyes and thoughts are to be elsewhere.

ALL EYES ON JESUS

What is interesting to me is how little the Bible talks about Satan. Sure, we have the book of Job, and a few miscellaneous references here and there, but overall, Satan is not spoken about much.

This is a clue that God never intended for us to *focus* on Satan or his warfare. He wants our focus totally and completely on Jesus.

> *"Let us **fix our eyes** on Jesus, the author and perfecter of our faith, who for the joy set before him endured the cross, scorning its shame, and sat down at the right hand of the throne of God." Hebrews 12:2 N.I.V.*

> *"Therefore, holy brethren, partakers of a heavenly calling, **consider Jesus**, the Apostle and High Priest of our confession..." Hebrew 3:1*

How do we know if we are focusing on Satan more than Jesus? Are we setting our minds on Jesus if we believe that Satan has the power to do as he wishes with Christians? Absolutely not. In fact, we are doing the exact opposite. We are fixing our thoughts on *Satan*, giving him the attention that he has always desired.

Which thought is more freeing and joyous: Jesus and His victorious work, or Satan hovering over you, poking at your mind with a demon rod? Of course the answer is Jesus and His work. The Bible says that truth frees us (John 8:32). This means that lies bind us up. So if a thought about Satan is binding you or distracting you from the truth, then it is a lie and is to be *rejected*.

Poor Ol' Job

Some of you may be thinking, "Wait, you mentioned Job. What about him? Doesn't Satan go to God to ask permission to attack us? I mean Job was stricken, wasn't he?"

This is true. Satan did a whole lot of damage to Job after he asked God's permission to do so. But we need to be careful in how we interpret biblical narrative. We can't say that because God allowed Job to be stricken, that situation must be happening all the time. We can't make a doctrine out of a narrative.

Think of the consequences if that idea was taken even further. We would all be casting lots to find God's will (Acts 1:26), and we'd be struck down dead for lying (Acts 5:1-11). Going back even further, we could all be slaughtering bulls and goats to make atonement for our sin, something that is Old Covenant (Leviticus). Narrative has a healthy purpose, but we need to be careful how it's interpreted. Just because Satan brought harm to Job *does not* mean that he currently has this power over believers.

Job lived before Jesus died on the cross, long before Satan was defeated. Job was afflicted before blood-bought saints had the power and Spirit of God permanently dwelling in them, and were irrevocably owned by God as His children (1 John 3:1). Because sin had not been obliterated for the believer, no one had an intimate relationship with God as we have today. He was no one's Abba except Jesus.

But Jesus defeated Satan. The evil one cannot bring direct harm to the children of God, or attach to them. He is a liar and the father of lies, and he throws those lies at us daily, but that's all he can do to those whom God owns.

Please notice what I am *not* saying. I am *not* saying that Satan does not wage war on believers' lives. He does. The battles we fight as humans are not ultimately against each other, but Satan. He uses people against the children of God in the form of persecution and other tactics. But nowhere in the Bible does it say that Satan has control or power over believing individuals under the New Covenant.

Think about it. If this really were a problem, wouldn't God have found it a good idea to include some instruction in one of the epistles? I can see it now:

Dear Timothy,

Regarding the poor brother who keeps getting demon possessed, it is necessary for you to immediately cast holy water on him while reciting the Lord's Prayer. After precisely five splashes (not one less) you must grab him and shake him violently until the little devil is gone or until a migraine has begun. Command all the brethren in this practice.

To keep this from happening again, please tell him to keep from dancing too close to that girlfriend of his. She is bad news. Oh and grace and peace to you and our dear afflicted brother.

Best,
Paul

Of course I'm being facetious, but hopefully you can see my point. The epistles do not give us instructions like this. Instead, the emphasis is placed on Christ and His finished work, powerful enough to break any demonic stronghold at the moment of salvation.

So we know that Satan's work in believers' lives is extremely limited, but that it is real. We also know that we can tell whether a statement about life or spiritual warfare is from God or not based on whether it frees us or binds us.

So if spiritual warfare is a reality, what can we do to defend ourselves against the lies of Satan? To understand this, we need to look at our armor.

Battle Strategies

- When we focus too much on Satan, we become distracted from the finished work of Christ. This "over-focus" is especially tempting when we face the inner battles with sin that we all experience. But it is crucial to remember that we are not free from the *presence* of sin. We are free from its *power.* We still struggle with impure thoughts and while these may be from Satan at times, they can come from directly *within* us.
- Keep Jesus and His finished work in focus. When you experience spiritual resistance, don't try to analyze it. Simply thank Jesus for victory and rest in His finished work. You are safe and secure in His arms, and His power is more than enough to break any demonic stronghold at salvation.

Seven

The Stand

stand
[stand]
verb

1. To stop or remain steady on the feet
2. To take a position

Paul is absolutely clear: spiritual warfare is a reality. In fact, it is *the* war behind all other wars that we see daily.

"For our struggle is not against flesh and blood, but against the rulers, against the powers, against the world forces of this darkness, against the spiritual forces of wickedness in the heavenly places." Ephesians 6:12

Our battle as humans is ultimately not against one another. We are simply caught up in a war between God and Satan. God has His children, and Satan has his. God has His truth that He speaks to all who listen, and Satan has his lies that deceive all who will believe them. Yes, even our culture is a battleground.

When love and truth are spoken and freedom through Christ is proclaimed, it is all God. But when our identity gets caught up in looks, money, sex, acclaim, or other manifestations of emptiness, it is all Satan. Don't believe for a minute that he is not behind the appeal of all things other than God. This is his plight and has been since the beginning.

As we look at our armor we need to understand something crucial: Christians do not fight *for victory* in the war. We fight *from victory*. Jesus defeated Satan (Colossians 2:15), and through our faith in His finished work Satan loses his hold on us. We are adopted into the family of God, with God as our Father and advocate (Romans 8:31).

But Satan is still around, and while the Bible does not tell us to fear him, it does speak of the importance of being *aware* of him.

"Be of sober spirit, be on the alert. Your adversary, the devil, prowls around like a roaring lion, seeking someone to devour." 1 Peter 5:8

Satan is defeated and we are victorious, but we must be aware that he is still working against us. Notice that John does not tell us to be frightened of Satan or to fear him in the way that we fear (obey) God. This is a position that God alone has in our hearts. But we need to realize that Satan does hate us and will do anything he can to get us to believe lies about God and ourselves.

The good news is that his lies paralyze and discourage, so we can recognize them. We can be alert to exactly what we believe and the effect it is having on us.

STRONG IN HIM

God has also provided a ready defense for us against the workings of Satan, and He has provided great armor that is ours for the taking. God's battle plan for us is simple: be strong, not in ourselves, but *in Him*.

*"Finally, be strong **in the Lord** and in the strength of His might. Put on the full armor of God, so that you will be able to stand firm against the schemes of the devil." Ephesians 6:11*

I used to read this verse and think, "Okay, got to get to work to put on the full armor of God. I need to find the armor through right behavior. What do I need to repent from? What do I need to change?" But that's not what it means to be strong *in the Lord.* That's how we become strong *in ourselves,* which is not the way to go with anything spiritual. The reason that the armor of God is so amazing is that it is sent directly to us from Him. Our Father's armor is a sure defense against the Devil's plans.

It is important to realize that we do not create our armor, and we can't find it by looking really hard. It is readily available to us only because of the work of Jesus. Whether Jesus is enough for our victory will be determined by how much we think we have to do to be safe from the Devil. Do we rest in Christ, or do we fight on our own power? Do we place faith in our moral behavior to keep us safe, or is it Jesus who has our faith?

SUIT UP

The armor of God consists of several components. Paul highlights the first few here.

"Therefore, take up the full armor of God, so that you will be able to resist in the evil day, and having done everything, to stand firm. ¹⁴ Stand firm therefore, HAVING GIRDED YOUR LOINS WITH TRUTH, and HAVING PUT ON THE BREASTPLATE OF RIGHTEOUSNESS, and having shod YOUR FEET WITH THE PREPARATION OF THE GOSPEL OF PEACE..." Ephesians 6:13-15

We "gird our loins" with the truth of God, which we find both in His word and in the voice of His loving Spirit. He guides us into all truth about Himself (John 16:13) and is always here to gently teach us, love us, and give us the "light yoke" of the gospel (Matthew 11:30).

Next we put on the breastplate of righteousness. It is easy to look at this verse and think that it's about righteous and moral living, but remember we are being strong in *the Lord*. It is *His* armor that we are putting on. Not ours. So whose righteousness are we talking about? It is the righteousness of Jesus Christ that has been given to us as a free gift.

> *"He made Him who knew no sin to be sin on our behalf, so that we might become the **righteousness of God in Him**." 2 Corinthians 5:21*

Our righteousness is *never* from ourselves. It is always from Him. So whose righteousness are we putting on? In a sense it is ours, and we need to own this precious gift. But it does not have its origin within us. It has its origin in Christ. He is our righteousness. If we cling to our righteousness in Christ, Satan will never be able to distract us from our identity.

Next we wear Christ's good news, "the gospel of peace," on our feet. Nothing makes us ready to fight the enemy more than knowing and living from our peace with God. No matter what accusations Satan throws at us, no matter what lies he tells us, we can remember our peace is with our Savior. No longer is there a division between God and us. Jesus took care of this. So we can boldly say that no matter what trial we face, *we are at peace with our God.*

These "armor truths," when combined with faith, help us to destroy all attacks from the enemy.

> *"...in addition to all, taking up the shield of faith with which you will be able to extinguish all the flaming arrows of the evil one." Ephesians 6:16*

We must have faith (trust) in these truths in order to experience their reality. Notice I did not say that we must have faith to *make* them a reality. They are already real for Christians. But we won't *experience* the truths of God unless we trust in them. When the lies of the enemy are coming at us, and he is saying how worthless we are or how little God loves us, or how angry the Almighty is with us, we can extinguish those arrows with faith in the truths we know, which are contrary to these statements.

Lastly, we put on our favorite helmet, and take up the sharpest sword.

> *"And take THE HELMET OF SALVATION, and the sword of the Spirit, which is the word of God." Ephesians 6:17*

The helmet of our salvation is our ultimate, eternal deliverance from death. It protects our *minds* with the truth that no matter how badly we mess up or how hard our lives get, we are forever saved and will one day experience salvation from this world. Until then we use the word of God, His most precious truth, as our sword. The Holy Scriptures teach and remind us of the truths of God. It is where we learn about God Himself. This is why it is so important that we study and know Scripture – not out of some religious "duty," but so that we can learn exactly who God is and what we have in Christ.

After we have put on our armor, we need to stand.

> *"Therefore, take up the full armor of God, so that you will be able to resist in the evil day, and having done everything, to **stand** firm." Ephesians 6:13*

Standing firm against the lies of this world can be tiring. We have all experienced intense seasons of hardship and spiritual resistance, times when God's love and truth feel as distant as the sun or moon. But in all of this we must stand firm.

No warfare occurs needlessly. God only allows battles and struggles into our lives in order to shape us and stretch us. Then, when our "spiritual workout" is done, He lifts us, restores us, and confirms us (1 Peter 5:6-10).

GOD IN THE SPOTLIGHT

We don't need to be anxious when we are afflicted spiritually. We only need to see it as God lovingly investing in us. The author of Hebrews puts it this way:

> *"Endure hardship **as discipline**; God is treating you as sons. For what son is not disciplined by his father? If you are not disciplined (and everyone undergoes discipline), then you are illegitimate children and not true sons." Hebrews 12:7-8 NIV*

Discipline is not the same thing as the "punishment" our earthly parents exerted on us as children; Jesus has already taken the punishment for our sins. Rather, divine discipline *prepares us for the rest of our lives.*

God does not allow a trial to enter our lives unless He can purposely use it for our good and future glory (Romans 8:28). So when you are tempted to freak out over the warfare in your life, thank God instead for the hardship. Know that, ultimately, it isn't warfare from Satan that you are experiencing. It is *strengthening* by God.

Sure, God may allow lies from the Evil One to penetrate, but it is just one other way that our amazing God has defeated Satan. He takes Lucifer's *best* tactics and uses them for our good. He takes spiritual attacks and makes them into discipline. We must always keep God in the spotlight with warfare.

The issue of spiritual warfare is a hotly debated, huge battle in the war for grace. But the bottom line is this: Jesus' work is either enough for our total victory over Satan, or there is a lot of work to be done in fighting him. Ephesians 6 makes it clear that Jesus' work is enough, and that all we need to do is put on the armor that God has for us. This is all we need to stand firm in Christ.

His work is the only defense we have against the enemy and the only true weapon in the fight for grace. He needs to have center stage in our lives so that Satan does not grab our attention.

After we have put on our armor, we need only to stand. We can boldly, in faith, proclaim Jesus in the midst of our battles, standing on top of what He has done. He is our true victory over Satan. *He* is our weapon.

Battle Strategies

- There is a battle going on all around us as Satan tries to wreak havoc on the world that God created. For the Christian, Satan's chief weapons are lies, especially lies about who we are in Christ. Because of God's great love for us, He has provided us with a ready defense against these lies. This defense is the armor of God.
- While some churches teach that the armor of God is about Christians making sure that *their* behavior is in check, it really has nothing to do with us. It has everything to do with *Him.* The armor of God is a gift from God, the reality of all that we possess in Christ.
- As you encounter lies in your daily life, place your faith in this armor. When you feel dirty or sinful, place your faith in the reality of your righteousness in Christ. When you feel as though you are not at peace with God, trust in the gospel of peace that has made you forever right with God. As you place faith in these truths, you can stand no matter what lies the Evil One throws at you. His truth in Christ is the only weapon that you need.

Eight

180

1. A bee line outta hell

There it was, glaring at me. Directly below the "What do I need to do to be saved?" column in our church bulletin were the words "Repent and turn from your sins," listed as one of several steps that a person must go through before they could truly believe.

I had grown up with this idea for so long that its meaning failed to sink in at first. But the more I looked at it, the more I began to see a serious problem: *How can someone truly turn from their sins before they believe in Jesus?*

You may not see the problem at first, either. It may seem like the "180-degree turn" from sinful behavior to right behavior is a natural step on the path to faith. But look at the process of repentance for salvation as it's defined above; it's not only unnatural, but impossible. The idea gives the false impression that we have the power to change ourselves, a concept completely contrary to grace.

Faith in Jesus' finished work on the cross is necessary *before* we can begin to approach the idea of turning from our sinful behavior. We need to be set free before we can do a "180."

A War of Nature

In the film *What About Bob*, Bill Murray's character, Bob Wiley, says that there are two types of people in the world: those who love Neil Diamond and those who don't. While I see his point, I think that people's identity runs a tad bit deeper than this. Scripture also says that there are two types of people in the world (without mentioning Mr. Diamond). There are those who are spiritually dead and those who are spiritually alive.

Every human being is born spiritually dead because we inherit Adam's sin.

> *"Therefore, just as through one man **sin entered into the world**, and death through sin, and so **death spread to all men, because all sinned**..." Romans 5:12*

Original sin eventually brought Adam and Eve physical death. But another death occurred as well: the death of their spirits, the eternal part of what it was to be human. Part of the miracle of becoming a Christian is not simply that we have our sins forgiven (as if that wasn't wonderful enough), but that we come back to life.

> *"When you were **dead** in your transgressions and the uncircumcision of your flesh, He made you **alive** together with Him, having forgiven us all our transgressions..." Colossians 2:13*

Coming to Christ means receiving new and abundant life. Our old selves are crucified and buried along with Christ, and we are raised to new spiritual life.

> *"...knowing this, that our old self was **crucified with Him**, in order that our **body of sin** might be done away with..." Romans 6:6*

For Christians, there is no need to strive to escape "the old man" or "crucify the old man" or "put to death the old man." The old, sinful us has been completely obliterated by Christ. At the moment of salvation, we became completely new creations (2 Corinthians 5:17).

But what type of state were we in before we came to Christ? We were spiritually dead and completely *enslaved* to sin.

*"And you were **dead** in your trespasses and sins..." Ephesians 2:1*

*"For when you were **slaves of sin**, you were **free** in regard to righteousness." Romans 6:20*

Part of being spiritually dead is being under sin's constant domination. What do spiritually dead people do best? They sin! Stop and think back to the time before you were a Christian. What was more dominant in your life: sin or righteousness? What sins dominated you? How much did you enjoy sin?

I loved it. I craved it. I could not get enough of it. Then I started hearing about this Jesus fellow and how He died for my sins. I knew it was the truth and trusted in Him for my forgiveness. It was only after this that I began gradually seeking God and feeling less disposed toward sin. Sure, I still sinned, but the sinful habits that I had before salvation slowly began to seem less appealing.

That happens because of the amazing change that occurs at salvation. As Christians we are set free from sin and are naturally bent towards righteousness.

*"...and having been freed from sin, you became **slaves of righteousness**." Romans 6:18*

We even have God's very own *nature* within us.

"For by these He has granted to us His precious and magnificent promises, so that by them you may become **partakers of the divine nature**, *having escaped the corruption that is in the world by lust." 2 Peter 1:4*

How did I realize that a change had occurred within me? It was because my entire spiritual anatomy changed. I went from being enslaved to sin to being enslaved to righteousness. Just as sin was natural for me before salvation, so righteousness was natural for me afterwards.

When Jesus Christ comes to make His home with those who believe in Him, they are set free from sin. But before this occurs, the unbeliever lives a different story because *sinful behavior cannot be helped or avoided when people at their core are spiritually dead.*

When believers come to unbelievers and tell them that they must give up their lives of sin in order to be saved, it's like telling a child munching on a lollipop, "I am going to give you your Christmas present. But before I do, you need to give up that sucker in your hand!" What would the child do? He would probably cry. That child loves lollipops!

If the Christmas gift is greater than the lollipop, you might be able to change the kid's mind about things, and getting him to give up his candy would be a less daunting task. Similarly, those who have not received salvation as a *free gift* have no reason to truly leave their sin nature behind. Sin's hold on the individual is not destroyed until salvation.

I remember hearing a well-respected pastor speak about all that must be given up to follow Christ. According to this man, it wasn't simple faith that saved. It was a person's total abandonment of their old way of life, as well as trust in Jesus as Savior. This type of gospel (if you can call it that) is a stronghold for those who oppose the gospel of grace. Their focus takes Christ out of His place on center stage and puts all of the attention on our behavior. It makes salvation about making ourselves pretty enough for Jesus to reach down and save us instead of acknowledging that Christ *makes us beautiful by His grace.*

Is abandoning sin a good action to take? Absolutely! But it cannot be done in order to receive salvation. That is why God does not require it.

BELIEF

It would be extremely hard, probably impossible, to find a Christian who will say that we are not saved through faith. The basis of Christian salvation is faith in Christ. The most famous verse in the bible, John 3:16, is all about belief in Christ. The Apostle Paul makes it clear that we are saved by grace through faith (Ephesians 2:8, Romans 3:26), and John spends more time talking about belief than almost anything else.

> *"This is His commandment, that we **believe** in the name of His Son Jesus Christ, and love one another, just as He commanded us." 1 John 3:23*

> *"He who **believes** in the Son has eternal life..." John 3:36*

> *"Truly, truly, I say to you, he who **believes** has eternal life..." John 6:47*

We see in Scripture that faith is God's tool for salvation. He promised Abraham that it would be through *faith* that He would bless all the nations (Genesis 22:17, Galatians 3:19). Nothing, not even the Law, could get in the way of His promise (Galatians 3:17). It has always been His plan to save people this way.

So what does faith mean? The Greek word simply means "to depend on or trust in." *Belief* comes from the same word. God requires people to depend on or trust in Jesus for salvation. What type of repentance is needed for salvation? Well, we know it has something to do with belief.

If repentance is a turning from sinful behavior to right behavior *in order to achieve salvation,* then the gospel writers did a pretty poor job of expressing it. If it takes more than simple belief in Jesus to achieve eternal life, then they should have spent much more time alerting people to this. Instead of saying that "whoever believes" has "eternal life," the apostle John should have said, "whoever believes and turns from their sins has eternal life." This is simply is not the case with salvation.

REPENT, REPENT, AND REPENT

There are three main words used for repentance in the New Testament: the noun *metanoia,* its corresponding verb form *metanoeō,* and the verb *metamelomai.* The first two words mean "to change a mind about something." Christians almost always associate the term "repent" with a change in behavior before God. But it can be used to describe any situation in which a person changes his mind.

I could easily say, "I am going to go to get a cheeseburger because it will really fill me up," and then *repent* and say, "Actually, I think a burrito would be more filling. I will do that instead!" What occurs is a change in mind from a *previous* form of thinking to a *new* form.

The third verb, *metamelomai,* typically refers to a change based in regret. If I decide to go get a cheeseburger one Sunday afternoon and experience a subsequent food poisoning, and then I make the decision to never eat a cheeseburger again based on the intense regret that I was experiencing (and it would be intense!), then I will have repented according to the use of *metamelomai.*

So how is each word used in Scripture?

Metamelomai is used to express regret based on a specific circumstance.

> *"But what do you think? A man had two sons, and he came to the first and said, 'Son, go work today in the*

*vineyard.' And he answered, 'I will not'; but afterward
he **regretted** it and went." Matthew 21:28-29*

*"Then when Judas, who had betrayed Him, saw that He had
been condemned, he felt **remorse** and returned the thirty pieces
of silver to the chief priests and elders..." Matthew 27:3*

*"For though I caused you sorrow by my letter, I do not **regret**
it; though I did **regret** it—for I see that that letter caused
you sorrow, though only for a while..." 2 Corinthians 7:8*

In each circumstance there is an event that leads to regret. In the parable of the two sons, the first son *regretted* his statement (probably based on some healthy guilt) and went to work the vineyard. Judas *regretted* betraying Christ and returned the thirty pieces of silver (Judas was never saved, by the way, according to John 17:12). Paul wrote a letter to the Corinthian church (1 Corinthians) that at first he *regretted* a bit, but ended up not regretting because it caused a lot of good for that church despite its harsh tone.

The greater debate over repentance arises over *metanoia* and *metanoeō*. There is a movement within the Church that suggests that true repentance will come only from a deep regret over sin and will lead to a true turning from sin and subsequent belief in Jesus. Charles Spurgeon was a believer in this. He said:

*"Repentance is a discovery of the evil of sin, a mourning that
we have committed it, a resolution to forsake it. It is, in fact,
a change of mind of a very deep and practical character,
which makes the man love what once he hated, and hate
what once he loved."*

Spurgeon understood a lot of great truths about salvation. He recognized that there was a change in internal nature that causes people to love the things of God and hate the things of the world.

But the fight over repentance is not about whether Jesus changes people. We know He does! It revolves around exactly what leads to this change and when this change occurs. Scripture is clear that it is not *conviction* of sin that leads us to turn to righteous behavior. It is Jesus' work in our spiritual *rebirth* that occurs at salvation.

> *"When you were dead in your transgressions and the un-circumcision of your flesh, He made you **alive** together with Him, having forgiven us all our transgressions..." Colossians 2:13*

> *"Therefore if anyone is in Christ, he is a **new creature**; the old things passed away; behold, **new things have come**." 2 Corinthians 5:17*

> *"...and having been freed from sin, you became **slaves of righteousness**." Romans 6:18*

So what type of repentance leads to this rebirth? This is the crucial question that we must answer. If it is a repentance that requires people to turn from sinful behavior to faith in Christ, then this opens up harsh standards that no one will be able to meet. But if it is something else, something simpler and more accessible, then we need to embrace it wholeheartedly.

Jesus Who?

We know that it is belief that saves, and that it is impossible for someone to truly turn from their sin apart from spiritual rebirth. So what repentance is needed for salvation? It is *a change in mind about who Jesus is and what he did.*

John the Baptist was the first person in the New Testament to bring this concept of repentance to the Jewish people who awaited their Messiah.

*"As for me, I baptize you with water for **repentance**,*
but He who is coming after me is mightier than I, and
I am not fit to remove His sandals; He will baptize
you with the Holy Spirit and fire." Matthew 3:11

The Jews were waiting for a military messiah who would deliver them from their Roman oppressors. God sent John as a forerunner to Jesus to help prepare the way and *change* the people's *minds* about the messiah that they were expecting. The Apostle Paul elaborates on John's purpose in preaching repentance.

"Paul said, 'John baptized with the baptism of
*repentance, telling **the people to believe in Him** who*
*was coming after him, that is, **in Jesus**.' "Acts 19:4*

John the Baptist helped willing Jews confess their sinfulness and their need for the coming messiah. It was this faith that the Jews, and later the Gentiles, would use to bring them back to spiritual life and pass from darkness into light. This was Jesus' command to Paul on the Damascus road.

"Now get up and stand on your feet. I have appeared to you
to appoint you as a servant and as a witness of what you have
seen of me and what I will show you. I will rescue you from
your own people and from the Gentiles. I am sending you
to them to open their eyes and turn them from darkness to
light, and from the power of Satan to God, so that they may
receive forgiveness of sins and a place among those who are
sanctified by faith in me." Acts 26:16-18 NIV

It is faith in Jesus that sanctifies us (sets us apart), and through this we are set free from sin and are brought back to spiritual life. It is because of Christ's work that we even have the power and desire to turn fully from sin. So it is preposterous for the Church to require people to have such a radical change in heart on their own. It is impossible to turn from sin without Jesus living within us, and this happens only through faith. So our concluding argument about repentance might look something like this:

1. Before salvation we are slaves to sin.
2. God saves us through faith in Jesus, not a change in behavior.
3. At the moment of salvation, we are set free from sin and made slaves of righteousness.
4. Therefore, the repentance needed for us to be saved and set free from sin is a change from unbelief to belief in Jesus.

FIGHT FOR THE SON

Obviously, the first step of being saved is confessing our sinfulness to God and trusting in Jesus. It is impossible for Jesus to save us unless we know what we are being saved from. But this does not necessarily mean that there will be a *regret* for sins committed, as Spurgeon and others believed. It means that there will be *recognition* of the need for forgiveness and a reception of it in Christ.

There can be an emotional response to our sinfulness that is regret (*metalemonai*). This *can* lead to salvation (*metanoia*) but is not *required* for salvation. All that is required is a change in mind about Jesus.

As born again Christians, we spend our lives renewing our minds and changing our behavior. Because sin has lost its hold on us, we can do 180-degree turns in our behavior, and this is a great practice! *But this is not the first step to salvation.* We must first be saved by Christ and empowered to leave sin behind through this salvation. Turning from sinful behavior to right behavior is only possible because the Son sets us free after we declare faith in Him.

Those who are enslaved to sin are naturally sinners. It is not until they recognize their need for Jesus' free gift of salvation that this can even change. When we as a Church clutter the gospel with ideas about repentance, and a journey to salvation that is more than trusting in Jesus, we ask people to give up what seems natural to them.

Jesus is not enough for us when we make salvation about anything other than dependency on Him alone. When we make repentance – or any aspect of salvation – about what we *do* instead of what has *been done* in Christ, we fail to fight for the Son, and we exchange His gospel for a second rate piece of trash.

This is why we must fight for Him. He is worth it, and the world needs the real Savior. So do you.

Battle Strategies

- The entire world is born enslaved to sin. Because of this, it is impossible for anyone to truly turn to righteous behavior before Christ sets them free at the moment of salvation. Often the Church puts the horse before the carriage, saying that part of becoming a Christian is turning from sin, even though it is impossible to do so until one is already a Christian.

- At the moment of salvation we are given new natures and made slaves of righteousness. We can do "180s" in our behavior all day long! But until the free gift of grace is accepted, this is not the case. "Acceptance" of the gospel is what it means to *repent* for salvation.

- As you tell people about the gospel, don't ask them to give up a sin that they are enslaved to; make sure that the gospel offer remains a *free* gift based solely upon trust in Christ. After salvation, you can help them understand their changed spiritual identity. Help them to see that they are no longer built for sinful behavior, and that they can powerfully live in freedom from sin.

PART 2

Fight for the Spirit

Jesus Christ did not just come to show us the way; He is the way. He did not just teach us some truth; He is the truth. He did not just leave us a manual to live by; He is our life. Whatever the need of the human heart, Christ offers Himself as the solution. His eternal answer is 'I am.'

Bob George

Nine

Abundant?

a·bun·dant
[uh-buhn-duhnt]
adjective

1. Present in large quantity
2. Well supplied

I attended two well-known Christian universities. Both, while miles apart in terms of political affiliation, had similar policies on chapel attendance. Students were required to attend services several times a week, and at each chapel there was a station where we had to check in. If we didn't attend enough chapels, we were penalized.

I was actually put on "chapel probation" at both universities. I loved going to church and celebrating God, but as soon as it became mandatory, it became a chore. I figured if I went to a forced chapel I would just end up doing my homework in the back like the rest of the students were, so I might as well stay in the comfort of my home.

My chapel truancy at the first college was a rebellion against the rules, and looking back I wish that I'd sucked it up and gone. The second college, though, was a different story. Chapel services there were more like political events than a time to celebrate Christ. Since I knew I would be leaving at the end of the semester, I stopped attending, thinking that it wouldn't matter. A few months later, I found out that I had a fine of something like $200 for not attending chapel! I was fined for not worshipping God!

Something is wrong. Somewhere in the fight for grace the Christian walk became a rule-keeping game, complete with its own point system. We ended up believing that while we are saved by a free gift, we needed lists of rules to keep us from "abusing" grace or getting too far off the "narrow path."

Rules are often made with good intentions. We want to keep ourselves in line, and we want to help others do the same. Christian colleges want their students to be God-centered, so they require chapel. While this might seem noble, rules like that are proof that something is wrong within the Church. When we're not excited enough about Christ to celebrate Him voluntarily, we feel like we have to set up spiritual boundaries to keep us from going off the deep end or moving away from God.

Too many Christians have a serious fear of freedom in Christ, but this is not our only issue. We also don't know the Person we should be celebrating with our lives. If Christians proclaimed and Bible teachers taught the pure, unadulterated gospel, I have a feeling that Christian college students wouldn't need to be forced to go to chapel. They would flock to services with enthusiasm, eager to celebrate their loving God with each other.

The same is the case with our lives as Christians. If we truly understood the God that we believed in and all that He has done for us and to us, then there would be no need for rules, because there would be joyous celebration all day, every day.

This is the difference between abundant life and rule-based moral living.

The First Rule Book

God created the first "rule book" for humanity. In fact, the entire Old Covenant was based around it. You may know it as The Law.

God created humans for relationship with Himself. We, of course, ran the other way, but He pursued us and chose Israel as His special people. God came closer to relationship with humanity than He had since the rebellion. But because God is perfectly righteous and just, and therefore hates sin, it wasn't as simple as God forgiving and forgetting the past. There needed to be boundaries and requirements for relationship with Him. This is where the Law came into play.

At Mount Sinai, God gave Moses the Ten Commandments, which showed God's perfect moral standard and what His people had to live up to if they wanted to be in a relationship with their Creator. Through the sacrificial system of atonement, Israel could stay in fellowship with God.

But the Law was not simply God's moral standard. It was also a tool to point out sinfulness. Paul elaborates in Romans.

*"Now we know that whatever the Law says, it speaks to those who are under the Law, so that every mouth may be closed and all the world may become accountable to God; because by the works of the Law no flesh will be justified in His sight; for **through the Law comes the knowledge of sin.**" Romans 3:19-20*

The Law showed how perfect God was, but it also showed the Jews – and ultimately the "whole world" – how far short they fell of this perfection. Humans saw the Law and exercised their own human effort to keep it, and they failed miserably. When we violated the Law, we violated God's standard.

The Law even excited sin, making it more prevalent. According to Paul, the Law didn't just produce one type of coveting. It produced every type.

*"For while we were in the flesh, the sinful passions, which were **aroused** by the Law, were at work in the members of our body to bear fruit for death." Romans 7:5*

*"But sin, taking opportunity through the commandment, produced in me **coveting of every kind**; for apart from the Law sin is dead." Romans 7:8*

Since sin is opposed to the Law of God, it guides people to violate this Law, and humans cannot overcome this battle on their own. At first glance that may seem like a cruel trick by our Creator, but a little perspective helps: the Law reveals our sin to us so that we can be saved through faith in Jesus.

But once we are saved, what part does the Law have in our lives as Christians? NONE! The Law was created to be fulfilled by humans. Humans could not fulfill it, so God did it for us.

*"For what the Law could not do, weak as it was through the flesh, God did: sending His own Son in the likeness of sinful flesh and as an offering for sin, He condemned sin in the flesh, so that the requirement of the Law might **be fulfilled in us, who do not walk according to the flesh but according to the Spirit**." Romans 8:3-4*

The Law is completely fulfilled in Christians. Because Christ is the end of the law (Romans 10:4), the Law finds its full purpose *in Him*. God fulfilled His own first rule book to make a point: we are ultimately not meant for relationships based on rule keeping. Yes, the divine rules had their place, but it wasn't to keep humanity on the right track forever. It was to point us to our Savior, so that we would live by *His Spirit*.

What place does the Law have in the world? It still holds the unbelieving world accountable to God. The Law is meant not for the righteous, but the unrighteous.

"We also know that law is made not for the righteous
but for lawbreakers and rebels, the ungodly and sinful,
the unholy and irreligious; for those who kill their fathers
or mothers, for murderers…" 1 Timothy 1:9 NIV

The Law is meant for those who have not received Christ. Christians are no longer under the Law. We are under grace (Romans 6:14). So what are we doing creating lists of regulations to keep us in line?

We are creating standards for ourselves that God Himself doesn't have for us. Where in the New Testament does God require worship in a chapel? Doesn't that defeat the purpose of worship? Isn't it supposed to be willing, not forced?

THE PROBLEM WITH RULES

When we make the Christian life about keeping laws and rules, we essentially create standards for ourselves that we will ultimately fail to fulfill. We may see success for a while as we follow our rules, but before long we will see our failures.

Rule-keeping spirituality ends up trapping people in this vicious cycle. We say through our words and actions that the Christian walk is about keeping certain rules. We then set up rules that we will ultimately break. Then we think we need more rules to keep from breaking the current rules, in order to keep us Godly. This produces even more self-focus and very little authentic zeal for Christ, which produces apathy, which leads to requirements for doing things that Christians should naturally do, such as attending services to celebrate Christ.

This lifestyle places *us* in focus, not Christ. This is the core of the problem with the Christian walk today. People aren't excited about Jesus because they see Christianity as a religion full of rules and spiritual disciplines. When being a Christ follower is about mandatory chapel attendance instead of the amazing work of the

Son on the cross, it is dead. We were saved to experience His life in and through us today, not to keep rules.

But What About Sin?

Don't rules keep us from sinning? I wish I had a dollar for every time I've seen this discussed. When people ask this question, there are usually a few key principles that they do not understand.

The first is who they are in Christ. Scripture shows us that after we are saved we are free from the power of sin and made slaves to righteousness (Romans 6:18, 6:20), and that we actually share in God's desires (2 Peter 1:3). This means that at our core, we do not want to sin. At our core, we desire what God desires. The Holy Spirit also lives in us and leads us to live like the righteous people we are (Galatians 5:22, 25).

Second, they don't understand grace. Because grace can be rejected and abused without it becoming compromised, people jump to the conclusion that without structure we will become hellions and abuse it. But this is not what Scripture says. Grace instructs "us to deny ungodliness and worldly desires and to live sensibly, righteously and godly in the present age..." (Titus 2:12).

God wants people who are not slaves to spiritual rules. He wants people who truly live the abundant life of Christ, and who are obedient from the heart. Earlier we looked at the forgiveness of God that is available to us in the New Covenant. But we skipped over a part. Do you remember it?

*"FOR THIS IS THE COVENANT THAT I WILL MAKE WITH THE HOUSE OF ISRAEL AFTER THOSE DAYS, SAYS THE LORD: I WILL PUT **MY LAWS** INTO THEIR **MINDS**, AND **I WILL WRITE THEM ON THEIR HEARTS**. AND I WILL BE THEIR GOD, AND THEY SHALL BE MY PEOPLE." Hebrews 8:10*

In this new way of doing things, God has written His laws on our hearts so that we obey Him from the inside out. We are slaves of righteousness (Romans 6:18) because God has written His truth on our hearts and minds. This is not the Law of Moses (remember, we are not under Law). It is God's righteousness written on our hearts, a righteousness that moves us to continually *believe* in Jesus, *love* one another, and that *predisposes* us to Godly living as God Himself moves within us (1 John 3:23, Ezekiel 37:26).

Sin is simply not an issue in the new covenant. God has taken care of it by changing our own desires to be like His. When we live for God, we do so authentically, not superficially. This makes all the difference in the world.

This is what is so great about how God has chosen to do things under the New Covenant.

AN ABUNDANT LIFE

Jesus promised abundant life. This type of life will never be found in our spiritual disciplines or requirements. It will only be found in living from His finished work within us. Jesus did not come to make a bunch of bad people good. He came to bring something that we lost because of the Fall: abundant life.

"The thief comes only to steal and kill and destroy; I came that they may have life, and have it abundantly." John 10:10

Have you ever thought of Christianity as the key to living life to the fullest? What about life as God has it? If you haven't, it is because you have been served a cold dish of Christianity instead of the beautiful feast that God intended it to be. Christianity is about knowing Jesus and experiencing *His* life within us through the power and presence of the Holy Spirit. It is about letting Jesus live *His* life through us and with us as new creations redesigned to live for God. *This* is what God intends for His children, not rules and regulations.

The battle for grace is not simply over the work of the Son at Calvary. It is over the person and place of the Holy Spirit in our lives. Somehow "the walk" has become less about knowing and experiencing this Spirit and more about doing things like church, Bible study, prayer, and so on. These are all beneficial practices, but they will become routine, failed disciplines unless we know who Jesus is within us.

Until we understand the Spirit and the abundant life we have in Christ, our version of abundant life will be making sure our weekly church attendance is in check. How dull is that?

Battle Strategies

- Jesus came to give us a life far beyond stagnant, ordinary, or bland. He came to give us *abundant* life, a life that *overflows* in its satisfaction and enjoyment.
- Oftentimes being a Christian doesn't seem like an abundant life. Instead of the joy of knowing Christ, we find rules and regulations that are meant to keep our spiritual walks in line. While these rules seem noble, they do not fit God's plan for our lives after salvation.
- God already used rules as a way to relate to humanity. These rules showed us how far short humanity falls in trying to meet His standards on our own. They also showed us our great need for salvation in Christ. But once we are saved, we are not meant to live according to spiritual rules. We are meant to have *relationship* with our God and *experience* the joy of His Spirit within us.
- Is your Christian walk full of abundant life, or are you playing the rule-keeping game? Take time to assess your walk with Christ. Ask Him to help you live the *abundant* life that He desires for you. Remember that at salvation you became a completely different person. God changed you from being predisposed to sin to being predisposed to righteous living. You don't need rules to keep you "in line." You can be who God has designed you to be.
- Deep down, you don't really want to sin. So rest, keeping Jesus' work in focus, and begin thinking about what it means to have the Spirit of God living within you. He is more than enough for your Christian walk.

Ten

The Third Person of the Trinity

per·son
[pur-suhn]
noun

1. A self-conscious and rational being

When I was a young Christian the idea of the Holy Spirit was confusing to me. Exactly who or what was this invisible thing? I knew that It lived in me, but I did not know why or how it had entered me. Maybe the description of the Spirit as the "Holy Ghost" added to my confusion.

I wish I could say that I completely understand the Holy Spirit now, but in many ways I'm still that confused kid. Perhaps I'm a bit more mature and knowledgeable of the Holy Spirit, but He still proves to be a mystery. Just who is this God who lives within?

GOD THE THIRD

Those who follow the religion of Islam object to the idea of the Holy Spirit, because they see the idea of one God in three persons as impossible. After all, how could one God exist in three distinct persons, including One who died on a cross and another who lives inside His believers? As Christians, we have to extend a bit of sympathy. The doctrine of the Trinity is odd, and the Holy Spirit is one of the main ingredients of this oddness.

Scripture says that the Spirit has been around since the beginning of all things.

> *"Then God said, "Let **Us** make man in **Our** image, according to **Our** likeness; and let them rule over the fish of the sea and over the birds of the sky and over the cattle and over all the earth, and over every creeping thing that creeps on the earth." Genesis 1:26*

Notice that from the very beginning God is not a singular person. He is *plural.* Some scholars argue that the "us" and "our" in the passage refers to heavenly beings, such as angels. But a close read reveals that humans were made in the image of whoever is being discussed here. And humankind was very definitely made in God's image.

The Holy Spirit was intimately involved in our lives from the very beginning. He was pre-existent, a creator. He existed before Jesus ascended to heaven. He has always been here. Jesus even alerted His disciples to the presence of the Spirit in their own lives.

> *"...the Spirit of truth, whom the world cannot receive, because it does not see Him or know Him, but you know Him because He abides **with** you and will be **in** you." John 14:17*

Jesus told His followers that the Spirit had been with them all along, but that something better was coming. After His atonement and ascension, the Holy Spirit would come to live inside them. I'm sure that this shocked them. Imagine Jesus telling you that someone you've never met will come and live inside of you. How would you feel? I would be a bit concerned. But because the Holy Spirit is real, this amazing truth is a reality.

The disciples would find out that this Holy Spirit was not a foreigner; they already knew Him intimately because they knew Christ, who would be the very One who would come to them.

"I will not leave you as orphans; I will come to you." John 14:18

The disciples were anxious. They were about to lose their teacher and greatest friend. Jesus comforted them with words that He knew would remain with them. They would not be alone for long. *He* would come to them in the Holy Spirit. Paul sheds even more light on this.

*"Because you are sons, God has sent forth the **Spirit of His Son** into our hearts, crying, "Abba! Father!" Galatians 4:6*

The Holy Spirit is not simply a cool thought or idea. He is the *Spirit of Jesus* living *within* the Children of God. He is Jesus in our world today. He is God's means of not leaving any of us as orphans.

A PARTY IN MY SPIRIT

My friend Lucas was starving for intimacy with God. For years, he'd found God during Sunday morning worship. Lately, however, the worship services were not meeting his need. Every Sunday morning he would show up craving an up-close-and-personal experience with the Divine, but every morning he would leave empty.

Lucas complained about the song choices, the worship team enthusiasm, and the church leadership, but still no change occurred that satisfied his need. I am not sure what state Lucas is in today, but I can identify with him.

I, too, have spent time seeking intimacy with God, believing that I was the closest to Him when I felt His awesome presence and love. When I was a younger Christian, I had these experiences often, and they were great. But when they weren't there I thought God had backed away from me.

Like Lucas, I felt God the most during musical worship on Sunday mornings. I came to church expecting to feel God and be close to Him. If I didn't feel close, I thought it was the song choice, or the worship team, or something from my own long list of critiques. But the reality was that it had nothing to do with any of these things. It had to do with *me*, and how I viewed intimacy with God.

Sometimes our feelings do not match reality. The Bible refers to our feelings, emotions, thoughts, and wills as our souls, which can be all over the place in terms of experience. It is in our souls (from the Greek word *psychē*) that we feel stress and anxiety, panic and fear, joy and happiness. Jesus promises rest to our souls (Matthew 11:28-30). But our souls are not our guide to truth; what we feel does not match with reality all the time.

No Christian has any cause to think they are distant from God simply because they don't feel close. It is impossible for believers to get any closer to God. Through the Holy Spirit we have *all* of Him within us *all* of the time. Take a look at one of Jesus' last earthly prayers to the Father.

> "*The glory which You have given Me I have given to them, that they may be one, just as We are one; **I in them and You in Me**, that they may be perfected in unity, so that the world may know that You sent Me, and loved them, even as You have loved Me." John 17:22-23*

Notice anything peculiar about this passage? Jesus does not simply say that one person of the Trinity will be in the disciples. He says "…that they may be one, just as **We** are one; **I** in them, and **you** in Me…." He says something similar to a disciple named Judas (not Iscariot).

*"Jesus answered and said to him, "If anyone loves Me, he will keep My word; and My Father will love him, and **We will come to him** and make **Our abode** with him." John 14:23*

You do the math. Jesus is in us, and the Father is in Jesus, so where is the Father? In us! *We have the entire Trinity living within us.* There is a party in our spirits, and we're invited to rest in our unending, uninterrupted intimacy with God.

As we focus on the amazing truths of the Holy Spirit within us, we begin to experience rest and peace. But the truth of God's presence in our lives through the Holy Spirit often evades us when we seek to get closer to God. After all, how often do we ask God to be with us?

Failing to understand this truth leaves us with a partial gospel that minimizes Christ's work for us. If we believe that God is an "on again, off again" Father who is sometimes with us and other times not, then it's not hard to begin thinking that we need to do things in order for God to be closer to us. Maybe we should confess sin, kneel while praying, go to another Bible study, or some other discipline of choice. When we come to conclusions such as this, we shrink the importance of Christ's work, and we end up performing penance in order to get closer to God.

This mindset can be summed up in the following argument

1. I do not feel God
2. God is not here if I don't feel Him.
3. I want God to be near me.
4. I need to *do* something in order for Him to come back.

Doing in order to gain God's approval or acceptance is another stronghold for those opposed to grace. If we are not fully united with God as believers through the work of Christ, then His work is not enough and we need to get to work. This is the "gospel" of every major Christian cult in existence. For the Jehovah's

Witnesses and the Latter-Day Saints, Jesus is not enough. They preach "Jesus plus good works" in order to achieve the best place with God. Are we as a Church better representing cult ideas than our own God?

Christians can't get any closer to God than we already are. Jesus Himself says that we are one with both Him and the Father. The apostle Paul agrees with this awesome truth.

> *"But the one who joins himself to the Lord is **one spirit** with Him." 1 Corinthians 6:17*

Deep within us, at our cores where our eternal spirits exist, we are one with Jesus. In fact, God can't tell where we end and Jesus begins.

ALL MIXED UP

I think a lot of Christians believe that we are like oil and water with God. We can try to mix the two substances, making them compatible, but it will never work because oil and water are non-cohesive materials. Like magnets when the same sides face one another, they are repelled. But this is not the case.

My wife and I love powdered chocolate milk. Both the chocolate and the milk are separate substances, having their own separate characteristics. But when they mix, they become one. I would give a person a million dollars (if I had it, of course) if they could accurately tell me where the chocolate ended and the milk began. This is the same miracle that has spiritually occurred within us. At salvation when the Spirit of Jesus comes inside the believer, we become like chocolate milk. The Apostle Paul puts it this way:

> *"For you have died and your life is **hidden with Christ** in God." Colossians 3:3*

When powdered chocolate and milk come together, they each give up something of themselves to become an entirely new creation. Jesus *gave* up His place in heaven to come to earth to die for us, and we *give* up our lives by being spiritually crucified and spiritually buried with Him.

"Therefore we have been buried with Him through baptism into death, so that as Christ was raised from the dead through the glory of the Father, so we too might walk in newness of life." Romans 6:4

The miracle of the gospel is that God has come closer to humanity than ever before. He is so close, in fact, that we are no longer like oil and water with Him. We are one, and we never have to ask Him to be with us because He is already closer than we could ever imagine. And He has promised that He will never leave us or forsake us (Hebrew 13:5). The work of His Son guarantees it.

True Spirituality

So how do we experience intimacy with God? We trust in the reality of His Spirit within us and walk in faith. If it was all about *feeling* God, then how much faith would we really need? After all, I know someone is there when I sense him or her in some way. But that's not a walk of faith. It is a walk of *experience*.

God does not promise that we will always feel Him, but He does promise that we can always experience His peace and joy, no matter what is happening in our lives. This is true spirituality.

"…for the kingdom of God is not eating and drinking, but righteousness and peace and joy in the Holy Spirit." Romans 14:17

When we are not experiencing these truths of the Holy Spirit, we are not trusting God's truth and we forget grace. This is why we must fight for the Spirit. Without His truth in our lives we will be hopelessly confused.

Battle Strategies

- The Holy Spirit is not simply a thought or a cool idea. He is a member of the Trinity who lives within the Children of God and is with us all day long. But more than this, through the Holy Spirit the *entire* Trinity lives in us. As mysterious as this sounds, it is completely true.
- When you feel distant from God, resist the temptation to do things in order to get closer to Him. Take time to rest in Christ's accomplishment on the cross and thank God that you are totally right with Him no matter what, because Jesus' blood is enough.
- Instead of *doing* in order to feel intimacy with God, simply place your faith in the *fact* of His presence within you. He has made you perfectly compatible with Him. So rest knowing that God is closer than you could possibly imagine, and that He wouldn't leave you.

Eleven

The Helper

help·er
[hel-per]
noun

1. One who gives support or aid

T he disciples were terrified. Their rabbi had just told them that He was going to leave them. For three years they had been away from their families and professions for Him. They were destitute and uncomfortable. Now they would be without their teacher, and all He would tell them was that He had bigger plans than they could even imagine, and that He would come to them in the person of the Spirit (John 14:8).

It is hard to imagine exactly what the disciples felt or thought when they heard Jesus. Most likely it was confusion. I mean, really, how could they imagine something as powerful and amazing as the Holy Spirit, especially against the image of losing the Man who had loved them so faithfully? Yet Jesus' words about the Spirit were meant not for confusion, but comfort. He was about to give them something that was literally out of this world, something that would allow them to do more than they had ever done, something that would drastically change their relationship with God forever. Jesus was going to give them His Spirit.

SPIRIT OF TRUTH

Before He died, Jesus gave the disciples a glimpse of their future partner.

> *"I will ask the Father, and He will give you another Helper, that He may be with you forever..." John 14:16*

That Helper, the Holy Spirit, came to the believers in power on the day of Pentecost. The book of Acts describes it like this:

> *"When the day of Pentecost had come, they were all together in one place. And suddenly there came from heaven a noise like a violent rushing wind, and it filled the whole house where they were sitting. And there appeared to them tongues as of fire distributing themselves, and they rested on each one of them. And they were all filled with the Holy Spirit and began to speak with other tongues, as the Spirit was giving them utterance." Acts 2:1-4*

It is hard to imagine. Jesus' intimate reunion with His disciples began with a "violent wind." Disciples began speaking in different languages as the Spirit enabled them. It was not long before this time that Jesus had described the Holy Spirit as the Helper, or *paraklēton*, from the Greek word *paraklētos*, meaning "comforter or intercessor." This "Spirit of truth" would glorify Christ by leading His disciples into deeper truth and explanation of who He is and what He did.

> *"But when He, the Spirit of truth, comes, He will guide you into all the truth; for He will not speak on His own initiative, but whatever He hears, He will speak; and He will disclose*

to you what is to come. He will glorify Me, for He will take of Mine and will disclose it to you." John 16:13-14

Today, we have the very same Being. The moment a person believes, the Holy Spirit permanently indwells in them as a new Child of God (Ephesians 1:13). The Helper comes alongside God's children all day, constantly counseling, instructing, and consoling by helping them to remember the truths of God, particularly the accomplishments of Christ.

He glorifies Jesus by magnifying His accomplishment on the cross.

THE GREAT SCORE KEEPER

The Holy Spirit is painted by some churches and Christians as "the great score keeper," keeping track of our failings and successes every day, making sure that we know when we've blown it. But is this the picture of the Holy Spirit that Scripture paints? Hardly.

The book of Hebrews offers insight into how the Holy Spirit views our sins, and more importantly, how He sees the work of Christ. Referring to the New Covenant, the author says that a time has come when God forgets the sin of all believers (Hebrews 8:12).

But the author does not stop there. He clarifies by saying the *Holy Spirit* has done the very same. The Holy Spirit's place is to glorify the work of Christ.

*"And **the Holy Spirit also testifies to us**; for after saying,*
'THIS IS THE COVENANT THAT I WILL MAKE
WITH THEM AFTER THOSE DAYS, SAYS THE
LORD: I WILL PUT MY LAWS UPON THEIR HEART,
AND ON THEIR MIND I WILL WRITE THEM,'
He then says,
*'AND THEIR SINS AND THEIR LAWLESS DEEDS **I***
WILL REMEMBER NO MORE.'" Hebrews 10:15-17

Often we adopt what I call a "cat-o-nine tails" attitude, seeking to achieve humility before God by keeping track of our sins and beating ourselves up when we fail. This attitude was popular in the past with religious leaders, and it still exists today. But concentrating on our sins does not glorify the work of Christ. It is self-focused, not Christ-focused. According to the book of Hebrews, the most humble attitude we can take towards our sins is to *forget them*. Apparently, we are never more like God than when we develop a short memory about our sins.

Sure, that may not seem fair. Deep down, we may want to give ourselves what we deserve when we sin. But grace has never been about fairness. In fact, grace is not fair at all! That's what makes it so amazing. Because of Jesus' work, we can forget our sins the moment that we commit them – not because we deserve it, but because Jesus has done something amazing for us. This is what the Holy Spirit is concerned about us remembering, not our sins.

There are still obviously earthly consequences for sin that we must deal with. Sin breeds horrific consequences. If I flip out and decide to cheat on my wife, I would not avoid consequences to my marriage and my ministry. But God would not see my sins.

You may be thinking, "But what about John 16:8-9? Doesn't this passage say that the Holy Spirit convicts people of sin?" It certainly does.

*"And He, when He comes, will **convict the world** concerning sin and righteousness and judgment..." John 16:8*

This is the passage that believers go to when they talk about the Holy Spirit, and Scripture does say that the Holy Spirit points out "the world's" sin. This is unquestionable. But who is "the world?" The second half of the passage reveals this.

*"...concerning sin, because they do not **believe** in Me..." John 16:9*

Who is the world? All those who have not *believed* in Jesus. Christians believe in Jesus. Their sins are forgiven and forgotten. But those who reject Christ are guilty. They stand condemned because they have not believed in Jesus (John 3:18).

So if the Holy Spirit has forgotten our sins and doesn't point out our mistakes, then exactly how does He help us live rightly in our walk with God?

FRUIT OF THE GOD

Jesus said that unless we abide in Him and He in us, we will not bear fruit for God. It just will not happen as long as people are detached from the Holy Spirit, the very *source* of the fruit.

> *"Abide in Me, and I in you. As the branch cannot bear fruit of itself unless it abides in the vine, so neither can you unless you abide in Me. ⁵ I am the vine, you are the branches; he who abides in Me and I in him, he bears much fruit, for apart from Me you can do nothing. ⁶ If anyone does not abide in Me, he is thrown away as a branch and dries up; and they gather them, and cast them into the fire and they are burned." John 15:4-6*

This passage is often used in the modern Church to describe the importance of remaining in Christ, as if it is a choice that we need to make daily. But we know that the Holy Spirit permanently indwells believers (Ephesians 1:13) and that God has promised to never leave or forsake us (Hebrews 13:5). So what was Jesus saying here?

He was showing the disciples the dire reality that, unless there was some way for them to permanently remain in Christ and vice versa, they would be "thrown away" and "burned." Without a Helper, Jesus said, the disciples would be lost.

He did not say it to scare the disciples, but to show them the necessity for God to provide a Helper. Jesus was not speaking with believers who were yet new creations and slaves to righteousness.

That happened *after* the cross. Here in John, the laws of God were not written on the disciple's hearts (Hebrews 8:10-12) because Jesus had yet to die, and the New Covenant had yet to begin. Jesus was introducing the New Covenant answer to this dilemma: His Spirit.

Notice that John 15:4-6 is sandwiched right between two passages about the promised Holy Spirit (John 14:16-27 and John 15:26-27). This is because the Spirit is the answer! Notice the famous fruit of the Spirit passage in Galatians.

> *"But the fruit of the Spirit is love, joy, peace, patience, kindness, goodness, faithfulness, gentleness, self-control; against such things there is no law." Galatians 5:22-23*

This passage reveals two important aspects of the Holy Spirit: it shows how He relates to us and how He lives through us. We never need to worry about how God acts towards us. He died for us when we were still sinners (Romans 5:6-8) and has a character that exudes this love towards us daily. The Spirit is always loving, joyful, peaceful, patient, kind, good, faithful, gentle, and self-controlled towards us. Because He exudes all of these characteristics, He constantly guides us to demonstrate these characteristics daily.

When we become Christians we express Jesus. It's easy to fall into the trap of believing that the Christian walk is all about us getting to work. But Christ said that we cannot bear fruit apart from Him, because He is the one producing the fruit. The Christian walk is not about being loving or joyful or patient on our own strength. It is about expressing the love, joy, and patience that He is *already producing* within us.

Grace does not only exist as God giving us the free gift of forgiveness and a ticket to heaven. It also exists in God's gift of the Holy Spirit. The Father did not simply send His Son to be our atoning sacrifice. He also sent His Son to dwell in our hearts to help us on the journey.

All too often we reject grace by making our Christian walks about "getting to work for Jesus" in our own strength instead of the strength of the Helper. We focus on the spiritual disciplines. We try and bring out more fruit and Christian character by going through a list of spiritual "do's and don'ts." But the reality is that we don't need any disciplines. We have Jesus in us, wanting to express Himself *through* us.

The Helper is our greatest ally in the fight for grace. He reminds us of Jesus' work and gives us what we need to live the Christian life. He is the Spirit of Jesus in us, living through us all day long.

Battle Strategies

- We were never meant to live the Christian life on our own; this would be impossible. Jesus knew this and sent His Spirit as a "helper" for us. The Spirit produces the "fruit" or character that we need to live for God.
- The Spirit is not here to condemn you or point out your sins. He has *forgotten* them because of the work of Christ! The Helper is here to remind you of this work and to produce the fruit that you need for the Christian walk.
- Situations come up throughout our daily lives that demand our immediate response. In these situations, learn to *rest* in God's unconditional acceptance of you whether you react correctly or not. As you rest, trust in the Holy Spirit to produce the character that you need in the moment (Galatians 5:22).

Twelve

Real Life

re·al
[ree-uhl, reel]
adjective

1. Existing as fact
2. Authentic

A t the first church I ever attended the leaders of the young adult ministry did something amazing. They created a group to help people understand the truth of the Bible and help them apply this truth to everyday life. It was not designed to make people more religious on the outside. It was designed to show us the relevancy and necessity of knowing Christ in the real world. The group was called Real Life.

I didn't realize the importance of the name until several years later. When they set up the group, the pastors decided they wanted attendees to understand something key about Christianity: knowing Jesus is not simply about getting a ticket out of hell. It is about meeting the Person who not only gives one purpose in life, but who is purpose itself.

"COME WITH ME IF YOU WANT TO LIVE!"

Most of us are familiar with the exploits of John Connor, the poor boy caught up in an epic battle with machines in the popular series of *Terminator* stories. In every movie, Connor is told that fate has chosen him to lead the human race to victory in a future war, which will start with Judgment Day. Despite any attempt to disrupt this future, fate always intervenes. No matter how hard John or anyone else tries, he continues on in his destiny.

Like John Connor, we know as Christians where we will end up eventually, but this does not tell us much about the relevance of knowing Jesus *now*. It's easy to look at what Scripture says about eternal life and assume that it is speaking only of heaven, the eventual destination for all believers. If this was true, we could receive the gift of eternal life now and put off letting our destiny impact our current earthly lives. But we would miss so much!

Imagine if John Connor chose to ignore everyone who told him about his destiny. Instead of being constantly alert for enemy terminators, John might have decided to commit his life to eating donuts, gaining weight, and becoming a machine rights activist. When fate finally called on Mr. Connor, he wouldn't have been ready. He would still serve his role (somehow), but somewhere along the way he would probably regret all those calories and protests.

There is a lifetime of experiencing *eternal life* that is available to all of us right now. Yes, heaven is an integral part of eternal life, and I for one am glad to be going there. But it is not the essence of eternal life. Eternal life is something that we possess from the moment we are saved and it never ends. This life is not merely the heavenly destination, but is *in* a very special person.

> *"And the testimony is this, that God has given us eternal life, and this life is **in** His Son." 1 John 5:11*

Eternal life is a gift from God that cannot be received apart from the Son. Jesus and eternal life are one and the same. They are a package deal!

This is why there is no way to see all religions as ultimately equal. No matter how hard we try to rationalize it, all spiritual roads will not lead to the same place. It is impossible for any person to have eternal life outside of Jesus. Jesus is that life. It is not a matter of choosing a religion. It is a matter of *knowing* God.

> *"This is eternal life, that they may know You, the only true God, and Jesus Christ whom You have sent." John 17:3*

The Christian walk is a relationship. It is a time to know God better and to seek to understand all that He has accomplished in Christ. So where are the rules? Where is the obedience? Apparently the only obedience needed for eternal life is obedience to the Son.

> *"He who believes in the Son has eternal life; but he who does not **obey** the Son will not see life, but the wrath of God abides on him." John 3:36*

How do we obey the Son? By believing in Him. We are given eternal life through simple faith.

So what does eternal life accomplish for us? We know that it is not just about heaven, but that it has to do with right now. So how does it apply to us today, this very moment?

GOD'S LIFE

A look at the original meaning of three Greek words will give us insight into eternal life: *apolētai* (perish), *aiōnios* (eternal), and *zōē* (life).

Some of you may recognize the three words from the most famous verse in the Bible.

> *"For God so loved the world that He gave His only begotten Son, that whoever believes in Him shall not **perish**, but have **eternal life**." John 3:16*

The Greek word for perish, *apolētai*, is commonly seen as a descriptor of hell, the final destination for unbelievers. While it does allude to hell in some contexts, its meaning is much deeper and more dreadful: to *perish* is *to completely fall short in finding and fulfilling God's purpose for life, and to consequently be eternally ostracized from His fellowship. Apolētai* describes hell as the final destination for those who have missed the *entire point* of life, for people who have not believed in Christ and therefore have completely missed the purpose of their lives! One simply cannot find meaning apart from Christ. It should be no surprise that so many are lost and confused in our world today.

Those who believe, on the other hand, have something far beyond wonderful. They have eternal (*aiōnios*) life (*zōē*). When these two Greek words are combined, the phrase means *to completely succeed at finding God's purpose for one's life, and to have life as God Himself has life*: a life without beginning or end, the life that the very Son of God has within Himself.

Just as hell is the natural consequence for all who are perishing, heaven is the natural consequence for people who have eternal life. But the destinations are not the whole story. Jesus wants us to have abundant life right now.

> *"The thief comes only to steal and kill and destroy; I came that they may have life, and have it abundantly." John 10:10*

As much as our Savior wants to be with us in heaven, He wants our experience of heaven to begin now through our relationship with Him. Our true purpose is in Him.

It's easy to worry about finding God's will for our lives. We often wonder, "Is this the right time to get married?" "Should I move to this house or that house?" "Should I take this job or that job, or go to this school or that school?" God speaks to us and offers us counsel and wisdom for all aspects of life, but we can rest in knowing that because we believed in Jesus, we have already *found* our ultimate purpose in life. There is no secret or hidden meaning for our lives. We exist to know Him.

KNOWING THE SON

So what exactly does it mean to know Jesus? What exactly *is* this abundant life?

We experience abundant life when we learn to place our faith in the truths that God has declared about His Son. When we accept that Jesus has truly done it all, and when we choose to cease striving to make ourselves prettier or better before God, we experience grace and life abundantly. When we choose to depend on the Spirit of Jesus within us to produce the fruit that we need in any situation, be it patience or peace, we are getting to know the Son and live abundantly. When we approach the Father with boldness in prayer, knowing that we will "receive mercy and find grace to help in time of need" (Hebrews 4:16), and when we experience the freedom of calling God Abba and trusting Him to give us what we need, we experience abundant life.

Knowing the Son means freedom, and freedom mean *real* life. This is not meant to stay a theological concept. We are meant to experience this real life right here and right now. The abundant life that Jesus came to give us is not about rules or Christian regulations. It is about experiencing the Holy Spirit of God in our moment-by-moment existence, learning to depend on Him for everything we need for our Christian walk. In Him we have received everything we will ever need in our spiritual lives.

*"...seeing that His divine power has granted to us everything
pertaining to life and godliness, through the true knowledge of
Him who called us by His own glory and excellence." 2 Peter 1:3*

Often may we feel as though we need to grow in our faith
so that we have more of God and are better disciplined in the
Christian life. But the reality is we already have everything we
need, because we know Jesus and have His Spirit within us. The
Christian walk is not about gaining more of Him, but growing
in our knowledge of what we already have. This is the abundant
life that Jesus promised. He has given us all of Himself, holding
nothing back. We are fully equipped to live the Christian life. We
need nothing else. Jesus is truly enough for our walk.

FIGHT FOR THE SPIRIT

Our eternal life has already begun, and it is not a life of rules or
spiritual disciplines. It is a life of Jesus Christ Himself living in us
through His Spirit. The more we get to know the God who dwells
within us, the less we will feel the need for rules to keep us in line
or make us go to chapel. We will not be able to contain the joy
within us as we learn how much He loves us and as we grow in
the knowledge of what He has done for us.

God did so much more than die for our sins. He pours Himself
into His children, adopting us into the family of God. Any
substitute is a point for the opposition in the war over grace.

Grace does not end at salvation or start after we die. Jesus did
not say, "It is accomplished; now you get to work." He simply said,
"It is accomplished." He has done it all on the cross and has fully
equipped us for the Christian life.

Is the reality of the Spirit's goodness in our lives worth fighting
for? I will let you answer that question.

Battle Strategies

- Eternal life is not merely about going to heaven. It is about *knowing* the resurrected Savior who dwells within us. When we believe in Jesus, we find our true purpose in life, and we are able to know Him through His Spirit.
- So often Christians worry about finding the will of God. But the reality is that God's ultimate will for us is that we *know* His Son. Once we have a relationship with Jesus, we can rest knowing that we have satisfied our ultimate purpose.
- Is knowing Jesus important to your spiritual walk? You may laugh and say, "Of course!" But consider whether He is the most important thing in your walk by looking at how much emphasis you place on doing stuff for God versus getting to know the Savior. Christians are spiritually made for good works (Ephesians 2:10). However, we are told to live *from* our relationship with Christ, resting in His finished work and allowing Him to live through us.
- The more we get to know the work of Jesus and the character of His Spirit, the more we experience this abundant life that Jesus came to give us. So how well do you know Him? Is knowing Him your Christianity, or is your faith more focused on doing religious things?

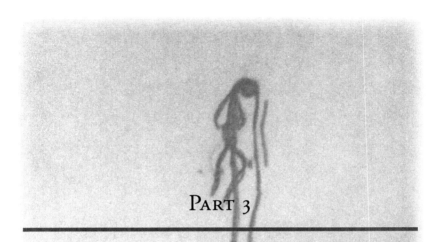

PART 3

Fight for the Father

Father! - to God himself we cannot give a holier name.
William Wordsworth

Thirteen

Dangerous Love

dan·ger·ous
[deyn-jer-uhs, deynj-ruhs]
adjective

1. Full of danger or risk; perilous; unsafe

Without the unconditional love of the Father, grace does not exist. So it's no surprise that this love is attacked in our world today.

There are many within the Church who view God the Father as a distant judge, unforgiving jury, and malicious executioner who wants nothing more than to jump on our backs with a riding crop and whack us into submission. Some pastors cast these unreasonable images of God on their congregations every Sunday morning.

While historically God has been a judge, jury, and type of executioner, it is far from the truth to paint His *character* as an overly critical and relentless taskmaster standing ready to give us a good beating. However well intentioned Christians who don't understand this may be, such teachings do more damage to the people's understanding of God than can be imagined.

GOD IS NOT TICKED

As I mentioned earlier, I was bullied quite a bit during some crucial years of my life. One day I was playing football against one of my biggest adversaries (we'll call him Slime Ball. Okay, maybe that's a bit harsh. We'll just call him Slime). I had the ball and was running toward the end zone when Slime tackled me. That wouldn't have been so bad, but that wasn't all he did. After I was down, Slime pushed my head into the grass in anger. I felt defeated, embarrassed, and naked.

This is the image we often have of God: a bully who chases us down, wanting to strip us of our self-worth. Once we are down, this bully God will give us a good ol' kick in the gut, just to make sure we know who's boss. But is this who God really is?

I don't ever want to make light of the holiness of God. He hates sin (evil) and will rightly condemn anyone guilty of sin to hell – this is part of God's just nature. But to say that His character is harsh is to completely miss the mark of who our Father is. He is not angry like Slime was. He is *love*.

In John's first letter he uses the Greek word *agapē* to describe the character of God:

> *"The one who does not love does not know God,*
> *for God is **love** (agapē)." 1 John 4:8*

This is a love beyond feelings and emotions, driven by a self-sacrificing nature. Paul expands on what this love looks like in the famous "love chapter" of 1 Corinthians 13. Check out the first few attributes:

"Love is patient, love is kind and is not jealous; love does not brag and is not arrogant, does not act unbecomingly; it does not seek its own, is not provoked..." 1 Corinthians 4-5

Now replace the word "love" with "My Father" and read it again.

"My Father is patient, My Father is kind and is not jealous; My Father does not brag and is not arrogant, does not act unbecomingly; He does not seek His own, is not provoked..."

Does this describe the Father that you know? Years ago, if I were to write my own description of God, it would look something like this:

"My Father is impatient. My Father is unkind. He waits for me to mess up so He can punish me. He is pleased with everyone else, but not me because I am not as good as everyone else. He gets ticked at me when I sin, and expects me to be perfectly behaved."

Sound familiar?

God is holy, perfect, and a hater of sin. But in the core of His being He is *love*. Love is in everything He does and in every way He acts towards us. Those who are not believers may still be under His wrath towards sin, and they may be condemned, but He will not act in an unloving way towards anyone. His character forbids it and demands that He chase after humanity in a love story unparalleled in all of human history. This is the Father behind the gospel of Jesus.

THE GREAT RISK TAKER

I've never been one for taking risks. In fact, if you ask those closest to me, I'm pretty sure that they would say I am a very cautious person, maybe even overly so at times.

When I met my wife Kristi, I was just coming out of a troubling time in my life which included the end of my first marriage and a subsequent two-year, soul-searching hiatus from dating. I'd spent my energy investing in my relationship with God. I'd done quite a bit of maturing and healing during that time, but I had intense seasons when I battled with whether or not I should ever take a chance with a relationship again – not just for obvious emotional reasons (I was totally prepared to head the next generation of celibate priests), but also for spiritual ones.

I had (mostly) learned to be content with having nothing but my relationship with God, but every so often I would get a sense that life would be fuller if I had someone to share it with. This thinking brought me to my knees one day, praying a simple prayer to God. It went something like this:

Father,
I think I'm ready. You know better than I do, but if it's in your will, I would like to meet someone.
All the best,
Andy

A week later I met Kristi.

She showed no interest in dating me, so I realized right away that she was not going to be an easy catch. I would have to pursue her. So I did. I took special interest in her when I could and made every effort to let her know that I thought she was special. Even so, when I invited her out a few times I got no satisfactory response.

I continued to hang out with her in groups, and even rode two roller coasters (I hate roller coasters). It took a little over a month of pursuit, but she finally agreed to hang out with me one on one. Our romance blossomed, and before I knew it we were on a fast track to marriage, her graduate education, and my first youth pastor position.

After all my time away from dating after my divorce, I took a chance. I found this gift of a girl, and risked myself for love. It took sacrifice then, and marriage takes more sacrifice now than I imagined. Those who have been married for decades tell me this does not change. Sacrifice and risk make up the very essence of love.

To try to describe the love of the Father is to make a vain attempt to explain something that the Bible says is above knowledge, and thus ultimately unknowable. That doesn't mean that we must be ignorant of whether the Creator of the universe loves His creation, but that we as humans, living in the finite, cannot possibly grasp exactly how *immense* His love is for us. The Apostle Paul elaborates on this:

"And I pray that you, being rooted and established in love, may have power, together with all the saints, to grasp how wide and long and high and deep is the love of Christ, and to know this love that surpasses knowledge—that you may be filled to the measure of all the fullness of God." Ephesians 3:18-19 NIV

The knowledge of this love that is beyond knowledge ultimately leads to maturity. Knowing this love, or not knowing it, makes or breaks us as humans. The problem is that knowing it takes tremendous risk.

We were all raised in our own worlds and come from our own unique religious backgrounds where we seek to find significance. Perhaps for some of us that means going to church, serving at the local homeless shelter, watching movies, listening to music, sharing our ideas and opinions, sewing, swimming, or – like one or two of us – it's the tiring pursuit of identity in achievement (okay, maybe it's more like three or four). To admit that none of these things ultimately lead us to lasting fulfillment, or even go with us when we die, is unsafe, gutsy, and very true.

It's astounding how many people walk this planet, coming and going daily, and yet never allow themselves to admit that they are unfulfilled – that the dream job wasn't exactly what they thought it would be, or the raise wasn't quite enough. We as a human race struggle with contentment and yet, somehow, we usually end up looking for it in all the wrong places.

How unsafe it is to admit this! There are so many stigmas attached to the simple admissions that we do not have it all together and that we have not found the meaning that our hearts crave. And that's preposterous, once we realize that we're all thinking the same thing.

I once sought meaning in relationships. I was the king of hopeless romanticism and wanted nothing more than to love a girl and be loved by her. I really believed that the key to my ultimate fulfillment was having a girlfriend. After I accomplished that, it wouldn't matter what I did or where I went in life. As long as I had *her,* everything would be just fine.

I finally found the relationship that I longed to have. Six months later we were married, and a little under a year after that, we were divorced. The journey led me from California, to Oregon, and then back to California again, because neither of us had a clue what we really wanted or who we were. We knew that *something* was missing. We just didn't know what.

No matter what we admit, Pascal's "God shaped vacuum" screams inside each of us, and we try to fill it with anything but God Himself. I was a follower of Jesus during high school, when I met my first wife, and yet I had not yet learned the most valuable lesson: that it is the Father's love that gives me meaning. It is God's love, not another person's, that is *meaning* itself. It is God's love that is meant to satisfy this man.

After we separated but before the divorce, my wife and I were still working together in a small store. This was one of the single most painful experiences of my life. My marriage was in limbo, and I was waiting for her to make the final decision about whether we could continue. We would frequently pass one other in the store, each passing glance bringing a shock to my weary soul and reminding me how uncertain my life was at the time. My only escape was a dirty bathroom, where I fled daily to cry for God to take control and do His will.

This was the greatest risk of my life. No longer was I going to look to human love for fulfillment, but I was asking my Father to be my all in all. And it was in that uncertain season of in-between that He met me on the dirty bathroom floor, changing my life forever with a love that proved my worth to Him.

The love of the Father expressed through Jesus Christ is the foundation for grace. Knowing that we are loved as we are and loved where we are is paramount to understanding why Jesus did what He did. While we were "yet sinners, Christ died for us" (Romans 5:8). Not when we had our lives altogether, but when we were at our absolute *worst*. Jesus came to save us when we were absolutely dead in our sinfulness.

He takes a risk in loving me daily. Sometimes the love is returned, other times not so much. But divine love has never been dependent on what we do in return; God would never stoop to such a low, fickle human love. His love risks rejection. It risks our saying no. It always has and always will.

The love of the Father doesn't just search for a response. It demands one. If people truly understood just how much they were worth and what Jesus did to save them, there would be a whole lot more rejoicing around us. Church wouldn't be a sterile Sunday morning shindig; it would be a week-long celebration that culminates with a joyous Sunday celebration.

Why is it called the good news? Because we are loved. Why are we loved? Because of our irreplaceable worth in the sight of God.

A Love That Shows Worth

A few weeks ago my wife and I were sharing our living room (a good discipline, I think). I had just sat down after a long day and was ready to watch something on T.V. As I turned my show on, I heard her begin to play a video on her computer. I stopped to listen. It was a news story about a young girl who had, in an act of selfless bravery, pushed her baby sister out of the way of a speeding car. Her sister survived unscathed, while the little hero was hit by the car and injured, losing a leg.

Wanting to show a bit of this girl's heart, the news anchor asked her why she had rushed to save her sister. She paused, clearly shy. And then four simple, unsophisticated words rolled from her tongue. "Because I love her."

I was amazed at the selflessness of a mere child, and how simple it was for her to explain it. She saw worth in her sister, and she acted on it.

As I sat there, having forgotten entirely what I was going to watch on T.V., the little girl's words sank deep into my heart. And ever so subtlety, I began to hear a simple word: *Calvary.*

Calvary, the pinnacle of world history and the single most powerful expression of love that has ever been or will ever be. *Calvary*, the point in time when the passionate, all powerful God made Himself nothing, chasing after an estranged creation in the most intimate way imaginable, assuming their flesh and blood. *Calvary*, the time when the Almighty Lover of mankind proved His stubborn, uncontrollable love by being hell-bent on suffering death so that no one need perish. And why? Because He loves us. Period.

This is grace. Is it worth fighting for? Dying for? You bet.

But we as humans have a hard time receiving this kind of love. Deep down, we feel as if we must make ourselves worthy of God's love, or any love for that matter. I see this in myself when I have been unreasonable or rude to my wife. She's the most nurturing, caring person I know, and she loves me when I am at my absolute worst. I know when I cross the line, but my poor choice of words or actions has often already negatively affected her.

In those moments, I feel completely unworthy of her love for me. I know that despite my bouts of rude, fleshly behavior, she keeps loving, caring for, and forgiving me. Such love is almost unbearable at times, but in those moments I can either accept her love or reject it. The same is the case with the love of our Heavenly Father. There is no off and on switch with Him. He is all love, all the time.

The reason we can have such a hard time accepting God's love is because we have been poor receivers of it. As Christians we tend to focus on how much we need to love people and do all of these religious things for God, often thinking that it is selfish for us to take time to stop and ask God to reveal His love for us. But as the old saying goes, we cannot give what we have not received. Jesus taught this very truth to His beloved disciples.

> *"A new commandment I give to you, that you*
> *love one another, even **as I have loved you**, that*
> *you also love one another." John 13:34-35*

Good luck loving people without knowing the love of God for yourself. It won't happen. Our actions will often feel forced unless we are receiving and transmitting the *agapē* of God.

Grace is under attack because Christians have forgotten how to receive. The time to allow ourselves to be completely dependent and receptive of the dangerous love of the Father is now. Without it, grace is defeated.

Battle Strategies

- The image that people often get when they think of the Father is a scowling parent, constantly pointing His finger, a God who is pleased to judge and condemn whenever there is wrong doing. Thankfully, this image of the Father does not exist in Scripture. He is described as love. Yes, God is holy and righteous, a hater of sin and the all-competent judge of it. But His character is one of love. At the core of our Father is a God who cares too much about His wayward creation to sit idly by. His love demands a pursuit to save all the people that He can.

- When you think of the Father, do you picture a parent who is constantly giving you a disapproving look, or one who is offering a giant smile that says "I love you"? The Father loves the whole world, sure. But do you believe that He loves you, just as you are?

- Because you are His child, the Father has poured His love into your heart (Romans 5:5). By doing this He made a commitment to loving you fully and intimately for all eternity. He has also forgotten your sins (Hebrews 8:10-12) which means that nothing can come between you and Him ever again. So the next time you feel like the Father doesn't love you because you sin or make a mistake, allow the Spirit to remind you of the Heart that was behind Calvary. The Father who sent the Son to loudly proclaim, "I love you."

Fourteen

Abba

Ab·ba
[ab-uh]
noun

*1. An intimate Aramaic word used by Jesus Christ
as an expression of intimacy towards God
2. Daddy*

My parents divorced when I was twelve, and both my parents were in new relationships within six months. This is a tough thing for any child, no matter what their age. But for a twelve year old, on the verge of entering into his teens, it was devastating. The teenage years are some of the toughest developmental years even without problems at home, but add to raging hormones the ever-present insecurity of divorce, and you have one troubled kid. I remember feeling an extreme sense of aloofness.

The hardest part was knowing that I had no control over what happened. I did not want my parents separated. They were my foundation. But instead I had to adapt to two new and different lifestyles in two separate homes, which brought out a lack of security in me. No matter where I was, I felt lost and unsafe, desperately in need of a new foundation. Desperately in need of a loving hand.

I found Valley Church in Vacaville, California a few years after the divorce. It was here I met the people who would forever change not only my view of God, but my entire concept of family.

THE BOY WHOM GOD LOVED

After quite a bit of resistance, I finally agreed to go to my friend Daniel's youth group. It was called Airborne then (now it's R.E.M.I.X.), and that's where I met my youth pastor and now close friend, Jeremy.

I'd never heard anyone talk about the love of God the way Jeremy did. I had trouble accepting God's unconditional love back then, and relentlessly asked him about whether I could ever lose my salvation. I just could not accept this concept that God's love *forbade* Him to let go of me. I had never experienced anything as safe and secure as the thought of a God who would never abandon me, a God who I didn't need to pursue, because He did all the pursuing.

Not long after I met Jeremy, I met another man who would also change my life: my small group leader, Tim. I remember the first night Tim was with us at Airborne. He had all of us line up against the wall so that he could take pictures that would remind him to pray for each of us throughout the week.

I was insecure about Tim's acceptance of me. I lined up with everyone else, feeling a little stupid and smiling at the bald guy with the big grin behind the camera. I didn't realize it at the time, but with the flash of Tim's camera I was adopted into a church family that would become one of the most powerful agents of the Father's love in my life. In this group I would meet my closest friends, and I would begin my journey of discovering God's love for me not simply as a Christian, but as a child. His child.

In order to grasp the otherworldly truth of our belonging in Christ, we must shove all of the mediocre, worldly examples of security out of sight and mind. All of the poor experiences with siblings, parents, and friends that may have caused insecurity must be set aside. For me, that was, and continues to be, a journey of not attributing my life experiences with *unfaithful* love to the God who is always faithful *to* love. He is not the grade school bully or the friend who betrayed me. He is not the parents who failed to love perfectly, and He is certainly not the spouse who left. His love is much bigger and bolder than anything that we could imagine. And this love offers true security for anyone and everyone willing to accept it.

Humans will *always* fail in loving us at some point, but The Father will never fail.

ABBA'S SON

In the night leading up to His crucifixion, Jesus was stressed and overwhelmed because of what He was about to endure. His disciples proved to be little comfort for Him. They struggled simply staying awake with Him through the night.

> *"Then He said to them, "My soul is deeply grieved, to the point of death; remain here and keep watch with Me. And He went a little beyond them…And He came to the disciples and found them sleeping, and said to Peter, "So, you men could not keep watch with Me for one hour?" Matthew 26:38-40*

Can you imagine the Son of God, alone on the night before the most painful experience imaginable? For any human this would be torture. And Jesus, every bit as human as He was God, must have felt the experience tenfold, because He knew that He was to be the last sin offering. He knew that He would *become* sin (2 Corinthians 5:21). Between the time when He left the disciples and returned to find them sleeping, He cried desperately to His Father.

> *"And He was saying, "Abba! Father! All things are*
> *possible for You; remove this cup from Me; yet not*
> *what I will, but what You will." Mark 14:36*

Jesus called God Abba. In the Jewish culture, the term "Abba" was used as a term of endearment to a father. It meant what "Dad" or "Daddy" means today.

This intimate relationship that Jesus had with the Father was nearly impossible for the religious leaders to comprehend. In fact, many viewed His approach to God as blasphemous and wanted to kill Him because of it (John 5:18).

To understand how intimate our own relationship with the Father is through Christ, it is crucial to see how Jesus Himself related to the father. The meaning is all in the term Abba.

ORPHANS

Jesus Christ's death, burial, and resurrection for our right standing with God are a necessary part of the gospel, but they are not the whole gospel. His life in and through us, today, is also a necessary part of the gospel, but even this is not the whole gospel.

We do not experience the whole, complete grace of God until we understand that we have been adopted. We belong to God. Even more amazing, He is *our* Abba.

> *"For you have not received a spirit of slavery leading to fear*
> *again, but you have received a spirit of adoption as sons*
> *by which we cry out, "**Abba!** Father!" Romans 8:15*

> *Because you are sons, God has sent forth the Spirit of His Son*
> *into our hearts, crying, "**Abba!** Father!" Galatians 4:6*

Before the cross Jesus called God Abba; after the cross, so can we. Why? Because we have been adopted by Him. At one point we were all spiritual orphans, born into this world separated from a relationship with God and in desperate need of Him. Jesus' work on the cross makes a renewed relationship possible in the most intimate way imaginable.

Too often we see Abba as unapproachable. At dark times in church history, such as the time leading up to the Protestant Reformation, the "common folk" were not allowed to read the Word of God for themselves. What type of picture did they have of God? It was not Abba. Man's religion has always sought to make the Father distant, but Christ's work has brought Him close. Jesus is our agent of *adoption*. It is through Him that we are adopted as sons and daughters.

> *"He predestined us to **adoption** as sons **through Jesus Christ** to Himself, according to the kind intention of His will, to the praise of the glory of His grace, which He freely bestowed on us in the Beloved." Ephesians 1:5-6*

> *"See how great a love the Father has bestowed on us, that we would be called **children of God**; and such we are. For this reason the world does not know us, because it did not know Him." 1 John 3:1*

It was God's plan from the beginning to provide a haven for spiritual orphans, a place where God was not a distant being looking down on earth, but where He was *Daddy*.

So what does this mean for our personal relationships with God?

> *"Therefore let us draw near with **confidence** to the throne of grace, so that we may receive mercy and find grace to help in time of need." Hebrews 4:16*

Jesus has paved the way for us, like Him, to boldly approach the throne of grace at any time to communicate with God. Whether in tough times or joyous times, or times of simple reflection and quiet conversation, Abba is always there to hear the words of His children. Being a child of the Almighty God certainly has its advantages.

Heir to the Family Business

My dad has always owned his own construction business. Because the company has a great reputation, he has stayed consistently busy for his whole career. It was this business, along with my mom's teaching salary, that provided support for me as a child.

When I was young, I remember my dad's employees asking me if I would one day take over the business. All I could think was, "No way, Jose!" I would never work full time in construction! They probably weren't serious when they asked me that when I was a kid, anyway, but it could have been a possibility. After all, I was my father's *son*.

My identity as my dad's son came with privileges. Even though I didn't want to spend my life working construction, I did end up working for my dad in various seasons. I knew he would always hire me if I needed it. I could go to him and ask him for work with confidence, knowing already what the answer would be.

Was this overly presumptuous of me, or was I simply confident in my dad's love and provision for me? I think the latter.

This is also the type of confidence that we can have with our Heavenly Father because of who He has revealed Himself to be. We can expect love from Him. We can expect Him to take care of us, whether or not we know what we need. Having Hebrews 4:16 confidence means we can approach God in boldness any time, day or night, and talk to Him about anything we want. Requests? Check! Thanksgiving? Absolutely! Just chewing the fat? Always allowed!

The only condition: the blood of Christ. Once the work of the Son has had its cleansing effect on us, all doors are wide open. Our relationship with God can be as confident as mine with my earthly dad. Jesus Christ went through hell for us to be able to approach God with freedom and confidence. I used to believe that God would only hear me if I confessed my sins, or if I did something really spiritual while I prayed, like kneeling. But the reality is that nothing is more "spiritual" than the work of Jesus on the cross. We cannot add to it or take away from it. It is everything.

God does not expect anything from us as we approach Him. He simply wants *us*.

BY OUR LIPS

A friend who is a pastor in San Diego once shared a thought with me. I had been really struggling with intimacy with God and was wondering if I was living this whole "Christian thing" right enough for God to have a relationship with me.

He said, "We don't have to try hard to get God to hear us. His ear is right by our lips."

He had no idea how much I needed to hear that. But Abba did. That day, at that very moment, Abba reassured me that He was close, He was listening, and I had every reason to boldly approach Him.

We hurt the image of the Father and fail to fight for grace when we teach that He is distant. Yes, God distanced Himself in the Old Testament from Israel because of their sin. But that was *before* the cross and *before* sin had been dealt with. There is no longer a reason for Him to be distant. Our sin is gone and our stable, secure relationship with God has come. Because of Christ we belong to our Father. I can think of no better truth for a used-to-be spiritual orphan like me.

Battle Strategies

- To say "God is love" is one thing. But to prove this love by saying that "God is Abba" is to proclaim the amazing truth of the believer's adoption into the family of God.
- Those who are not followers of Christ are alienated from a relationship with God. But once Jesus' work has been received, this alienation is annihilated and God becomes Daddy.
- So often this "Daddy" image of God is missing from our churches. The Father is portrayed not as Daddy, but as a ruthless judge. But the truth is all in the word Abba. Jesus, the perfect Son, called His Father Abba. And guess what? So can we!
- If you ever feel that you cannot approach the Father confidently, check what you believe about the finished work of Christ. If His work is truly sufficient and you have trusted in it, then approach Him boldly any time. Whether you have a request or simply want a conversation, approach Abba and let Him hold you. If you doubt His love, address Him as "Daddy" when you pray. This very well could change your entire perspective.

Fifteen

In Him

in
[in]
preposition, adverb, adjective, noun, verb

1. Inclusion

Growing up I was what some would call a movie freak. In high school I was "that guy" who had all the answers and best opinions about cinema. I had several *thousand* dollars worth of movies on VHS (remember those?) and DVDs. I also made movies for a hobby. I was "that guy" who everyone went to when they needed video projects for various classes. My friend Klotz thanked me multiple times for helping him pass a biology class because of an A+ on the video project. I liked that about myself. That was my identity.

We all search for identity in something. We all look for status in our fields and affirmation for our abilities. We want someone to see us for who we think we are, yet often who we think we are isn't really who we are at all.

The temptation in this world is immense to seek our identities in everything except for our relationship with God. Even as I write this book, I confess to the idea of becoming a well-known Christian writer who God uses to shape the future of the Church in a massive way.

Sure, this is a great dream. I would love to be used by God in any way He wants, and if this book helps people understand the true nature of God, then awesome! But what happens if it doesn't sell? What then? What if I only reach ten people instead of ten thousand? Is this less worthy of celebration than reaching the multitudes? It is if my perspective is skewed.

Every earthly identity that we put our confidence in will fade at some point. There will always be someone who is "better" than us or "above" our pay grade. Someone will always have more degrees than me. But the glory of grace is that the Father has provided us with a true identity in His Son, and it has nothing to do with external appearances. It has everything to do with our relationship to Abba through Christ.

CLEAN LIFE?

My wife and I enjoy the T.V. show *Clean House*. We love the characters and everything that they do for the guests on the show. But I've noticed that the homeowners tie their identities to the clutter of their homes. When the miracle workers show up and do their magic, the homeowners suddenly have this great hope. But I wonder what happens when the *Clean House* team leaves? Will the people keep their houses clean? Even if they do, will they continue to value their worth based on the cleanliness of their house? What happens if it burns down? What will their identity be then?

Through adoption, Abba has provided us with a final and secure identity that never changes. We are God's children through the work of Christ. We are associated with Jesus in everything. We are *in Christ*.

*"Therefore there is now no condemnation for those
who are in **Christ** Jesus." Romans 8:1*

*"...just as **He** chose us in **Him** before the foundation of the world,
that we would be holy and blameless before Him." Ephesians 1:4*

*"Therefore if anyone is in **Christ**, he is a new
creature; the old things passed away; behold, new
things have come." 2 Corinthians 5:17*

The Father has made it abundantly clear that everything good that we have, we have because of our identification with His Son. Our very identity as a Child of God is dependent on our relation to Christ (Ephesians 1:5-6), and we are hidden with Christ (Colossians 3:3). As Christians we only have one identity.

Today's culture seeks identity in everything from financial status to nationality. But the reality is that we Christians have no identity outside of Christ. Paul makes a powerful statement in Galatians supporting this fact.

*"There is neither Jew nor Greek, there is neither slave
nor free man, there is neither male nor female; for
you are all one in **Christ** Jesus." Galatians 3:28*

Ultimately we are not a nationality, a cultural status, or even a gender. We are "one in Christ Jesus." This is hard to grasp for those, like myself, who are in vocational ministry. My work is often so intimately connected with my love and passion for Jesus that it can be tempting to take "Pastor" as my first name.

I am proud to be an ordained youth pastor. I love teaching teens about Jesus because they are just rebellious enough to take Him seriously. But if I lose track of my identity in Christ, I go off kilter. Relational issues within the church hit me harder than normal because I care too much about what others think of me. My home life becomes affected as I struggle to love my wife in the way she deserves. I even become bound by my conscience, feeling guilty for any pleasure I may find in entertainment like video games (yes, I play those) or movies. When we lose track of who we are in Christ, any experience of freedom disappears. When we lose track of our identity, legalism abounds.

We begin telling ourselves "no" to things that are permissible under grace. We slowly allow the chains of legalism to take over, telling us what not to "eat" or "touch" or "play." And while such rules may seem like they are answers in the Christian walk, they do nothing to keep us pure (Colossians 2:23).

People who feel the need for spiritual rules to control their walks truly do not understand *who they are in Christ*. This is why identity is so crucial, and so attacked in the fight for grace.

Identity Unmasked

Identity is not exclusively a struggle for religious Christians. It is a struggle for every human being on earth. Since the days of Adam and Eve's fall in the garden, humanity's ultimate purpose has been lost in a clutter of pseudo-purposes that ultimately come up short. This is good and bad; it's bad in the sense that people will never be at peace apart from Christ, but good because the search for identity will continue, with the hope that all will find a true place in Christ.

Many people try to find identity by searching out a local church and attending for a while. Some of these people still go to church, while others may have been burned or rejected. But until we realize that it is a deeper issue than simply going to church or looking religious that makes up our identity, we will never find true identity in Christ.

Regardless of who we are, all humans are born with one identity. We are *in* Adam.

*"For as **in Adam** all die..." 1 Corinthians 15:22*

While many say that humans are made in the image of God, the reality is that after the fall, we inherited the image of Adam.

> *"When Adam had lived one hundred and thirty years, he became the father of a son in **his own likeness**, according to **his image**, and named him Seth." Genesis 5:3*

Regardless of who we may think we are as successful lawyers, wonderful parents, hoodlums, or even poor college students, we are either *in* Christ or *in* Adam.

We don't have a choice as to which family we belong to in the beginning. Because of Adam's sin, everyone is born into a sinful identity (Romans 5:19). Through Christ, however, we are adopted into a new identity. The Father takes us out of Adam and places us into Christ (Colossians 3:3). We are given a whole new identity and purpose.

THE FRUIT OF IDENTITY

I once heard about a boy who had been locked inside a closet for most of his childhood. This is no "Harry Potter" story. Apparently the boy had only known this lifestyle and thought that it was normal. He thought he was one of several thousand boys whose parents kept them inside a closet.

Imagine his surprise when he found out that not only was this not true, but that he was one of the *only* boys who grew up in a closet. How shocked would you be if you were this boy? How would you react if you found out that it was only *you* who grew up in a closet? What would you think about the people who claim to love you?

Self-perception is crucial to our lives on earth. We live according to who we believe we are, and our behavior is fueled by this identity. If our focus is on our looks, then we will be a slave to making sure our weight is where it should be, or that our makeup is always perfectly applied, or that our muscles are bulging enough. If our identity is in achievement, then the satisfaction of our life is dependent on how far we climb the ranks at school or work. If we believe that we are always meant to live in closets, then we will make sure every home we own contains one that is big enough.

But if our identity is in Christ, then this will change our perspective entirely. Instead of an identity found in a higher salary, we will be found in the unconditional love of God. Instead of caring about what everyone else thinks about our looks, we will only care what our Father thinks and find our identity in a love that does not change with weight or age.

Who we are as Children of God in Christ is at the heart of the fight for grace. Jesus cleansed us and gave us life because we became a part of something bigger than ourselves at salvation. We became ready to know God and be His hands and feet on this planet.

When our identity is attacked, we doubt who we are. We forget that we have been forgiven from sin (2 Peter 1:9), and we reject any notion that we are slaves to righteousness and actually desire what God desires (Romans 6:18, 2 Peter 1:4). We doubt whether we are close to God and wonder if He has abandoned us (1 Corinthians 6:17), and we miss belonging to Abba (Romans 8:15). We miss *grace*, and therefore, live from a wrong foundation and self-perception.

Identity is a treasure that everyone searches for in life, and sadly, many will never look for it *in* Christ. But Abba's children have found it revealed in grace, and this is something to be celebrated. This is something to own. This is something to stand up and fight for daily. We have to fight for who we are to the Father and stand by this fact if grace is to ever have a place in our lives.

Battle Strategies

- Everywhere we go there are false identities being thrown at us. Maybe you are a victim to one. Regardless of what you find your identity in, consider whether or not it has truly fulfilled you. If you are honest, you will realize that no identity outside of being *in Christ* is fulfilling.
- Take time to thank the Father for placing you into Christ and ask Him to help you fully understand this identity.

Sixteen

The Commands of God

com·mand
[kuh-mand]

Verb

1. To demand with authority

Noun

2. A decree given by a superior

The grace of God shown through Jesus Christ is under attack. By now, hopefully, you are beginning to see this. The truth about the Son is under constant scrutiny. The work of the Holy Spirit and the Christian life is under the same scrutiny. And our image of the Father has been largely skewed. The idea that "Jesus is Enough" is a hard one to grasp, but necessary.

You may be thinking "I see and understand what you are saying about grace. I get it! Jesus has done it all. But what do *I* do? Isn't there something that *I* need to do?"

Because the gospel is all about what God has done for us, it's easy to ask this question. We've looked at the importance of letting Christ live through us, and about understanding our identity and living from who we really are as Children of God. This is what we can "do" for God. But what does the Father expect of us? What *commands* does God have for us today?

We know that God *loves* us, but how do we *love* the Father?

A LAWYER'S QUESTIONING

Jesus was tested by the religious experts of the day quite a bit while He was on earth. They would try to trap Him in His words, hoping to prove Him to be a liar. Of course, Jesus was never a liar and always came up with the perfect answer to any question they offered Him.

One of the most intriguing conversations came from an expert in the Law of Moses, who Luke called a "lawyer."

> *"And a lawyer stood up and put Him to the test, saying, "Teacher, what shall I do to inherit eternal life?" And He said to him, "What is written in the Law? How does it read to you?" And he answered, 'YOU SHALL LOVE THE LORD YOUR GOD WITH ALL YOUR HEART, AND WITH ALL YOUR SOUL, AND WITH ALL YOUR STRENGTH, AND WITH ALL YOUR MIND; AND YOUR NEIGHBOR AS YOURSELF.' And He said to him, "You have answered correctly; DO THIS AND YOU WILL LIVE." Luke 10:25-28*

The lawyer asked Jesus what he needed to do for eternal life. Jesus' answer? Follow the Law. But Jesus takes it one step further. He says that love actually *fulfills* the Law. Love for God takes care of the commandments that are direct sins against Him (1-4), and love for one's neighbor takes care of the commandments that are directed towards people (5-10). So to fulfill the law *perfectly*, one must love *perfectly*.

As Christians in the twenty-first century, we can look at what Jesus said to the Lawyer and conclude that to love God today we need to love Him with all our heart, soul, mind, and strength. That's what they teach in church, that as Christians it is our duty to love God with "everything that we are." But notice something important about this passage. Jesus is talking about *eternal life* here, not a daily striving. Jesus is not talking about how people can love God in the day-to-day; He is talking about how to gain eternal life *under the law*.

Jesus did not say "believe in me" for eternal life. He said something that was in harmony with the Law. Why? Because he wanted to help the lawyer realize that to gain eternal life under the law, he would have to love God and others perfectly.

This is another example of Christ's ministry as it existed under the Law and how He strove to get the Jews to cease relying on the Law for righteousness and instead receive Him as their Savior.

We have already determined that Christians are not under the Law, which is meant for unbelievers (1 Timothy 1:9, Romans 6:14). So why would we apply this to our lives today? Can we expect to fulfill the Law any more than this lawyer? Of course not!

Hopefully by now we understand that the Christian has no relationship to the Law. If we apply this verse to our personal love for God, then we are putting ourselves under the entire Law, which is meant to show our sinfulness (Romans 3:20). So if we try to love God with all of our heart, soul, mind, and strength, we will forever be striving to attain a perfection that we cannot gain. If we travel this road, all we will find is how short we come in loving God perfectly according to the Law.

Does this sound like the desire of a God whose yoke is easy and burden light? No. And yet, in the battle for grace, we have adopted this idea into our spiritual lives, and in so doing have placed ourselves right back *under the Law*.

To love God perfectly, the lawyer had to *be* perfect. Thankfully, God has provided a much simpler way for us on this side of the cross.

THE TWO COMMANDS

The idea that Jesus is enough carries a lot of weight in the Christian walk. It makes us admit that we cannot do all of the religious things that we thought we could, and that those religious things that we've become accustomed to are not a part of God's will for our spiritual lives. *Even the idea of loving God is among these religious practices.* We are to have no relationship with the Law and, therefore, should not try to love God according to its standard. If we do, we will only fail, which is exactly what God means for us to do under the Law. Fail.

But the New Covenant reveals a way of loving God that is not burdensome. In the epistle of First John, the Apostle shows his readers the simplicity of loving God after the cross.

*"For this is the love of God, that we **keep His commandments;** and His commandments are **not burdensome**."1 John 5:3*

At first it may seem that he is referring to the Ten Commandments. But we know that this cannot be true since Christians are not under Law. We know also that these commandments John refers to, whatever they are, are not burdensome. (If you think the Ten Commandments meet that description, you're not trying hard enough to keep them). The Old Covenant was a burdensome covenant. So whatever this commandment is, it has nothing to do with the Law.

A closer inspection of the letter reveals what John is talking about. If you are eager to love God, then this is crucial to grasp.

> *"This is His **commandment**, that we **believe** in the*
> *name of His Son Jesus Christ, and **love** one another,*
> *just as He commanded us." 1 John 3:23*

We could never love God with *all* of our heart, soul, mind, and strength. But we can believe in the One who did. Honestly, what is more loving to the Father than receiving the awesome work of His Son? What is more glorifying to the work of Jesus than receiving it in all of its awesome glory and scope? There is nothing that makes the Father prouder than the work of His Son. Loving God means believing in Jesus and letting His work be all that it was meant to be in our lives.

The second command involves loving "one another." To love God, we love our brothers and sisters in Christ. This kind of love is a verb, not a feeling, that is to be acted on daily. But we do not need to come up with this love on our own. It is *within* us.

> *"We know that we have passed out of death into*
> *life, because **we love the brethren**. He who does*
> *not love abides in death." 1 John 3:14*

What is a sign that we are saved? We love the Church. How many non-believers love Christians? Not simply care about us as people, but embrace all that we stand for? I would say none. In fact, I would say that Christians are the most persecuted and hated faith in the world (maybe next to the Jews). The world hates us because we do not share its values (1 John 3:13). We don't speak its language.

So when someone receives Jesus and is born again and changed from the inside out, that person becomes a part of the family of God, and has fellowship or intimate friendship with this family (1 John 1:3). Sure, to love still requires a choice, but it becomes less burdensome because we have been reborn to love the people and truths of God.

FIGHT FOR THE FATHER

The Father does not want us to strive daily to love Him perfectly according to the Law. He has set up a far better system. He wants us to receive the One who did love Him perfectly, and to love our brothers and sisters in the faith like we have been spiritually redesigned to do.

The fight for grace revolves largely around the image of the Father. Is He truly a loving Abba who longs to bring us joy, or does He want to make our lives miserable? Is He a nurturer who loves without fail, or is He stubborn and temperamental? Is He out to make our lives burdensome, or is He here to give us rest?

Those opposed to grace make the Father seem like an unapproachable light who will do anything to complicate our spiritual lives. But the gospel says that what Abba wants more than anything is for people to see the finished work of His Son, and to believe that He loves us. Living for God is easy when we know what God we are living for.

The single hardest act in my life is to believe that God loves *me*. Not the guy behind me or the die-hard super Christian to my left, but *me*. And what is even tougher is trusting Him to love me on a daily, moment-by-moment basis through all of my screw-ups and victories, seasons of faithfulness and unfaithfulness, patience and impatience, and for Him to never see me as anything other than His prized Child.

If the church is to fight for our Father, we must accept Him as Love, while throwing away preconceived notions of what love truly is. We must travel back two thousand years in time to a Son who died so that His Father could redeem a lost and hurting world. It is true Love that compelled the Father to send the One and Only Son. And it is this love and the Being behind it that Jesus came to reveal.

Battle Strategies

- Religion says, "You must strive to love God with all of your heart, soul, mind, and strength. You must love Him perfectly and never cease in this striving until you do." The Father says, "I know you can never love me perfectly according to *the Law*. So love me according to *grace* by trusting in the One who did love me with all of His heart, soul, mind, and strength. Then love all of your brothers and sisters *in Christ* with the love that I *have given* to you. This is how *I want* you to love me. Nothing else will do."

- What if the most loving thing you can do for the Father is to receive the Son, and from this, love your brothers and sisters in *Christ*? As you fight the fight for grace, make sure that you are not striving to love God on your own. By doing this you place yourself right under the Law. Instead, glorify the work of Christ by trusting in Him and loving His other children. You will find no burden in these commands. Only grace, beautiful grace.

Conclusion

Why We Fight

Is Jesus enough?

Think seriously about your response to this. Your answer will determine what side you are on in the fight for grace and will show whether you are helping or hindering the gospel.

There is a daily struggle within all of us to live out a life of grace and let Jesus be enough. This is where the fight for grace begins – *within* each one of us.

We believers are the only gospel or Bible that many people will ever see or hear. Frightening, isn't it? You may be the only person who has the honor of telling someone about Jesus. So what will you tell them? Will it be an invitation into freedom? Or will you direct them on the path to the religion that you've always struggled with?

The fight for grace begins with *us*.

Is Jesus enough for me?

There once lived a man named Tshopo in a small village in northeastern Congo. He was considered the best local travel guide in the area, and people would regularly hire him as an escort to the surrounding villages.

147

One day a family on vacation from England hired Tshopo to take them on a tour of the sightseeing locations in the area. He agreed to take them on foot to the one of the largest waterfalls in the Congo, the Boyoma Falls. The family was ecstatic and agreed to leave early the next morning.

Shortly after sunrise they set out on their expedition. After several hours on the trail they came to a fork in the road and Tshopo called for a water break. The family sat down and rested.

After he had finished drinking, the young son of the family saw a path across from where they sat, going a different direction. "Where does this path lead?" he asked.

Tshopo wiped the sweat from his forehead and spoke in broken English. "To different falls. Most beautiful waterfall in all Congo."

Confused, the boy asked, "Why aren't we going to *that* waterfall?"

Tshopo looked down. "Many turns. Maybe get lost. I never been and don't know way. I can't take people where I don't know way."

It has been said that we can only take others as far as we are personally in our Christian walk. What happens if we do not understand the finished work of Christ? What if Jesus is not enough for *us*? Then He won't be enough to those we influence, at least not because of our ministry.

There is a dire need to enter the rest of God. The author of Hebrews puts it this way.

"Therefore let us be diligent to enter that rest…" Hebrews 4:11

*"For **we** who have **believed** enter that rest…" Hebrews 4:3*

Those who have received Christ have entered into a rest where works for righteousness cease and rest in Christ's finished work begins. We enter that rest at the moment of salvation and must learn to walk in that rest, asking ourselves daily whether we are allowing Him to be *enough*.

Human pride wants to add to the work of the gospel, and legalism only subtracts from its power. Those who allow either pride or legalism to influence their understanding of grace teach a gospel that is skewed and that ultimately distracts from the saving work of Christ. This is why we must fight.

We must let Jesus be enough for both our own sakes and the people who are looking for the freedom that the gospel promises. It simply is not an option. The world doesn't need more religion. It doesn't need more rules. It *needs* real life. It *needs* the Son who died for it. It *needs* the Spirit who longs to express Himself through it. It *needs* the Abba who cares for it.

The fight for grace does not consist of soldiers lining up with guns, ready to invade the enemy. Instead, it consists of a God who longs for the freedom of His wayward creation and who has done everything needed for it to be free. It consists of characters like Paul and John, who would rather die than cheat on grace. And people like you and me, who will humbly allow Jesus to answer our own longing for freedom so that we may be the modern expressers of His life.

Without grace and all that it brings, there is no gospel. And with no gospel, the world is forever lost.

There is something far better than man-made religion out there. There is hope. There is meaning. There is the rest that we all so long to have. And we *will* find it if we will only look to Jesus. In all of His greatness He waits patiently to pour His *grace* into our lives. We are all looking for some good news and it doesn't get any better than Him.

Discussion Questions

Part 1

1. The opening quote for Part One is "The burden of life is from ourselves, its lightness from the grace of Christ and the love of God" (William Bernard Ullanthorne). How does this quote reflect the fight for grace?

2. What are some areas in which grace has been stolen from your life?

3. Have you ever felt that you owe God something? Has this mindset negatively impacted your spiritual walk?

4. How might grace encourage Christians to live righteously?

5. What are some "benefits" of the New Covenant?

6. Where in Scripture does the New Covenant begin? How might this impact the way you read Scripture?

7. Is there anything that you do to try to remain forgiven with God? How does this impact your perspective on the finished work of Christ?

8. What has your experience with spiritual warfare revealed to you about Satan and his tactics?

9. Why is it so important to put on the full armor of God?

10. What does it mean to repent for salvation? How can getting the definition wrong negatively impact gospel outreach?

Part 2

1. Do you experience abundant life in Christ? If not, why do you think this is so?

2. How can spiritual rules get in the way of enjoying Jesus?

3. How many members of the Trinity live within believers? How might this impact your daily walk?

4. How much do you rely on the Holy Spirit to live His life through you on a daily basis? How might relying on Him greatly enhance your spiritual walk?

5. Have you ever thought of yourself as "compatible" with Christ? Why or why not?

6. Read Romans 14:17. Does this describe your spiritual experience?

Part 3

1. How is God a "risk-taker?" (See chapter 14)

2. Do you struggle with letting God love you perfectly? Why or why not?

3. Why is it unreasonable to think that we can love others without first receiving God's love for us?

4. What does "Abba" mean? How does it relate to our relationship with God through Christ?

5. What are some identities that you have assumed to find meaning in your life?

6. How does identity impact your daily life? Why is knowing who we are in Christ so important?

7. Have you ever tried to love God with all of your "heart, soul, mind, and strength?" How well did you do? Had you ever considered that this was a means of gaining eternal life under the law?

8. How do we love God in the New Covenant? (See 1 John 3:2)

Conclusion

1. What are some reasons why it is important to "Fight for Grace?"

2. What are some of the "Battle Strategies" from this book that have helped you be more equipped to fight for the gospel?

3. What are some of your own "Battle Strategies" that have worked in your walk with Christ?

4. Is Jesus enough for you?

Acknowledgements

I want to first acknowledge my wife, Kristi. I dedicated this book to you for a reason. Your encouragement in my life and during the arduous process of writing this book has been priceless. You truly are God's greatest gift of grace in my life.

I want to recognize my mom, Nancy. Thank you for making the decision to bring me into this world. Your love and encouragement is valued. So are you. I love you.

I would like to recognize my dad, Mark. Thank you for encouraging me to read the Bible. I don't know where I would be without the God that it reveals. I love you.

I would like to acknowledge Mike, Barb, Jeff, and Jason Eastman. I am so fortunate to have you as family. Jeff, you did an awesome job with the drawings for this book!

I want to recognize my dear friend Jeremy. Your presence in my life is irreplaceable. I mean it. Love you, bro!

I would like to give a shout out to all of my brothers/sisters/ mentors at Valley Church. There are too many of you to list by name, but just know that I am the person that I am today because of your faithful love in my life.

I would like to recognize the leadership and members of Mission Village Christian Fellowship, specifically Pastor Carl. Thank you for providing a warm and loving place for my family, and for giving me the room to grow as a leader. Also, to all the youth who have so lovingly and patiently allowed me to be their pastor: I love you guys more than you could ever know, even if you talk during announcements. Lastly, I would like to Acknowledge Russ Armstead. Your feedback has been wonderful. Thanks, my friend!

I would like to recognize my friend, Drew. Thank you so much for all of your encouragement and mentoring during this process. Your feedback and guidance have been priceless.

I would like to thank Beth Jusino for polishing up my book. You are a fantastic editor!

Last but far from least, I want to thank everyone at WestBow Press for partnering with me on this project. Your accessibility and creative expertise has made this a wonderful experience. I am proud to work with you and Thomas Nelson.

CPSIA information can be obtained at www.ICGtesting.com
Printed in the USA
BVOW031207240513

321597BV00010B/185/P